The Neophyte Rituals of Paul Foster Case

by Paul Foster Case

Edited by Wade Coleman

Copyright 2021 by Wade Coleman

June 2023 Edition

Upon my death, this book enters the
Public Domain.

ACKNOWLEDGMENTS

A special thank you to Carol Z for your editing.

To contact the author,

DENDARA_ZODIAC@protonmail.com

TABLE OF CONTENTS

INTRODUCTION	4
CHAPTER 1 – Opening and Closing	7
CHAPTER 1 – Notes	49
CHAPTER 2 – Ceremony of Admission	52
CHAPTER 2 – Notes	93
CHAPTER 3 – Equinox Ceremony	95
CHAPTER 3 – Notes	113
CHAPTER 4 – Implements and Regalia	114
CHAPTER 5 – Temple Setup	116
Paul Foster Case Books	122
Wade Coleman Books	123

INTRODUCTION

I began my magical career in Sacramento Pronaos. Wilt Chesterman came to one of our study groups and gave a lecture. Twice he said, "The dark forces are gathering." Soon after, he closed lodges. Wilt believed that humanity was not yet evolved enough to participate in group ritual work. At the time, I thought him an arrogant old man. Thirty years later, I see his point.

Many people are attracted to magical work to feel special or motivated to learn how to control people. However, every spiritual path, including the Western Mysteries, is a long slog of self-development and refinement. The Western Mysteries, and magical work in general, are not designed to make you feel special. Quite the contrary. As for control, a magical group is filled with strong-willed people. Running a lodge is a lot like herding cats. Any attempt to ram a hard sell down the throat of an initiate has a 100% chance of backfiring. I've seen it happen dozens of times, and each time the person is surprised that things didn't go the way they planned.

After decades of lodge experience, I have come to a more complete understanding of Wilt Chesterman's perspective. The magical organizations I've been involved in lack the checks and balances necessary to moderate large egos. You need a strong will to practice magic. However, just because we're confident we're right doesn't make us right. People, especially those in power, easily confuse the two. As my father would say,

"Just because your breath smells like ape shit doesn't make you Tarzan."

Most lodge conflicts can be solved if people take the summer off to de-escalate and meet back at the equinox. Instead, things escalate and end up with someone resigning or being forced out. The last words spoken to the departing initiate are inevitable: "RETURN OUR RITUALS."

However, the Paul Foster Case rituals are mostly Golden Dawn rituals. So much so that you cannot copyright them. Case rarely copyrighted his work, and his rituals are no exception. In this book, I have respectfully omitted the parts of the ritual that are unquestionably secret.

There will be those who think I've gone too far and broken my oath. However, I offer this perspective. The EA says this before the obligation. "After receiving my assurance that this obligation will bind you to nothing incompatible with your civil, moral, or religious duties, are you willing to take it?"

That's a big fat lie. Therefore, this oath violates my civil, moral and, most especially, religious duties. An oath of secrecy cannot be used to hide crimes and abuse people. That's against the law. My moral code is simple, if you're nice to me, I'm nice to you. If you're not nice to me, then I'm not nice to you. As for my Religious Code, my favorite hymn is "Onward

Christian Soldiers." My holy and sacred duty is to oppose evil in all its forms.

The Western Mysteries have been watered down, and the original meanings of the teachings have been forgotten or ignored in favor of Post Modernism and New Age ideals. All new lodges and their members must conform to the prevailing dogma, or they will be forced out with the demand to return "OUR RITUALS."

This is the 21st Century, and it's time for a new dispensation. Gone is the Piscean Age of conforming to dogma or facing ex-communication. Now is the Aquarian Age of enlightened rationalism. No organization *owns* the rituals. They are Paul Foster Case's gift to humanity.

CHAPTER 1

Neophyte Opening and Closing

I used abbreviations for the names of the Paul Case lodge officers. Some officer names are obvious. Others are a bit cryptic.

Ritual Floor Officers	
Paul Case	Golden Dawn
EA	Hierophant
A-n	Herius
A-t	Hegemon
H-r	Kerux
C-n	Dadouchos
P-r	Stolistes

Chiefs	
Paul Case	Golden Dawn
Pr-l	Praemonstrator
I-r	Imperator
C-s	Cancellerius

Visualizations

Floor Officer	Angel
EA	It depends
A-n	Sandalphon
A-t	Michael
H-r	Raphael
C-n	Raziel
P-r	Tzaphqiel

The C-n is the top of the Pillar of Mildness on the Tree of Life. The P-r is the head of the Pillar of Severity. The EA is generally Metatron to the A-n's Sandalphon.

As for the meditation before the lodge, look at Paul Case's Tarot deck for ideas. Some initiates are good at complex visualizations; I am not. Generally speaking, the best I can manage when performing a ritual is color.

For example, when I stand and speak my part, I'll visualize the color of my wings. When turning, I take a half step away from my chair so my wings don't brush up against my seat. When someone else is speaking, I'll visualize the color of their office as wings or a column of color from floor to ceiling. Everyone needs to be using the same color for each office. This builds the lodge egregore.

OPENING

ORATION

CRY OF THE WATCHER

1st DUTY

THE PASSWORD

THE SIGNS

SECRET NAME

ANTIPHONY

STATIONS AND DUTIES OF THE OFFICERS

PURIFICATION

CONSECRATION

MYSTIC CIRCUMAMBULATION

ADORATION

DECLARATION

MYSTIC WORDS

SIGNS

    Initiation Ceremony

RECESS

END OF OPENING

CLOSING

THE SIGNS

PURIFICATION

CONSECRATION

LIGHT AND SOUND

REVERSE CIRCUMAMBULATION

ADORATION

MYSTIC REPAST

MYSTIC WORDS

DECLARATION

END OF CLOSING

Similarities Between the Rituals

Golden Dawn and the Paul Foster Case (PFC) Opening and Closing Ritual are essentially identical.

1. Each initiate gives the semester password before entering the temple.

2. The ORATION, CRY OF THE WATCHER, and 1st DUTY are almost identical in the two rituals.

3. The officer duties are close with some modifications.

4. The PURIFICATION, CONSECRATION, MYSTIC CIRCUMAMBULATION, ADORATION, DECLARATION, and MYSTIC WORDS are the same in both rituals.

5. The GD and PFC Closing Rituals are almost exactly the same.

Differences Between the Rituals

1. In the Opening, the PFC ritual tests for the PASSWORD from the initiates, similar to the masonic tradition.

2. The SECRET NAME and ANTIPHONY are unique to the PFC ritual.

3. The step and the sign of silence are the same in both orders. However, the other sign of projected light sign is different.

4. In the Closing Ritual, the LIGHT AND SOUND work is unique to Paul Foster Case.

RITUAL OF THE 0=0
GRADE OF NEOPHYTE

HEBREW NAME: מתחיל[1]

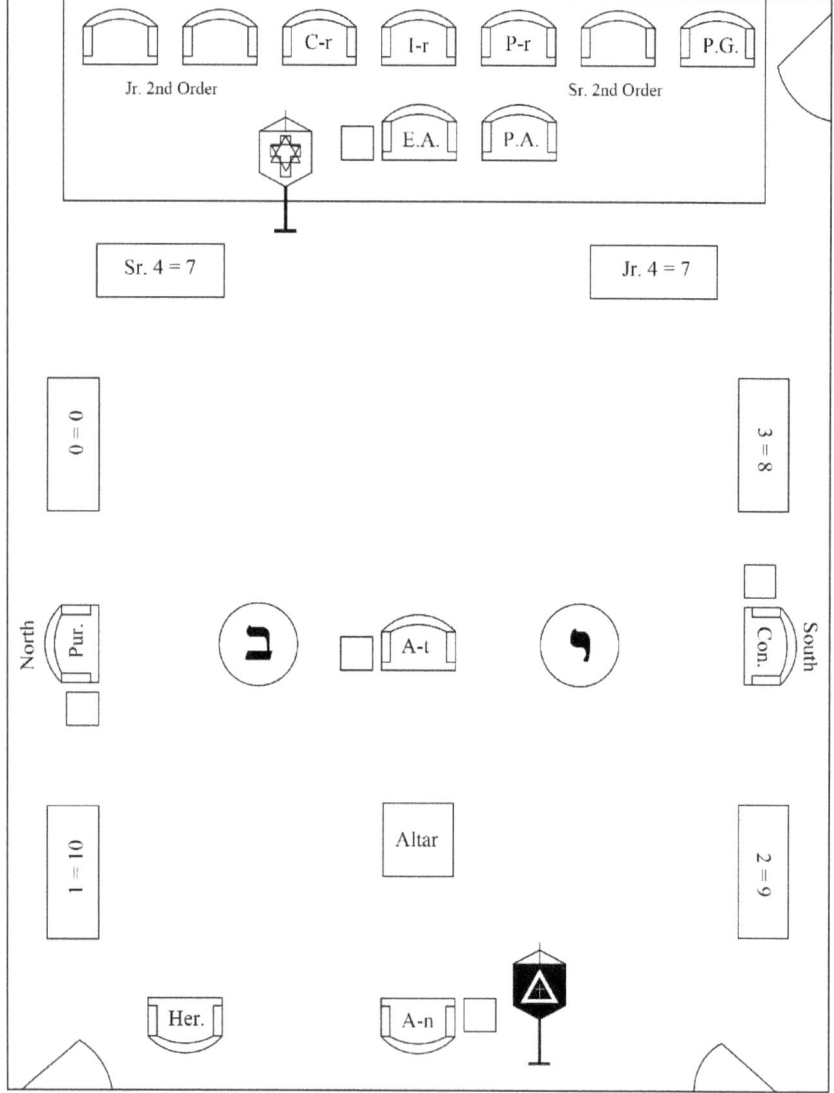

PRELIMINARY INSTRUCTIONS

All temples open in this grade. After the temple has been arranged and before the Lodge is opened, officers and members, clothed in robes and aprons, remain in antechambers. After outer court preparation is completed, members should sit and meditate. If there is an Inner Sanctuary, the EA, three Chiefs and other 2nd Order members prepare in this Inner Sanctuary, East of the dais. When no Inner Sanctuary exists, EA, Chiefs, and 2nd Order members may prepare for the convocation in any convenient place. None but the EA and H-r should enter the temple until called by the EA, except to perform a definite duty. When such a task has been completed, the member or officer returns to the antechamber and remains there until the EA calls the convocation.

When H-r has notified EA that all is ready and has opened the Portal, the members should line up for entrance. The order of entry is P-r carrying cup; C-n carrying censer; A-t, A-n, Senior 4=7, 0=0, 1=10, Junior 4=7, 3=8, and 2=9 members.

After entering, proceed to your stations and places and stand facing as usual.

When there is an Inner Sanctuary, the Senior 2nd Order members, Pr-l, and PA, enter by the S.E. door. At the same time, the Junior 2nd Order members, followed by I-r and C-s, enter by the N.E. door. They ascend the dais two by two steps, go to their stations and places, and remain standing.

When there is no Inner Sanctuary, the 2nd Order and Chiefs enter from the antechamber before 1st Order members have reached their places & stations.

The Order of Procedure for all convocations is as follows:

1. Opening
2. Initiation (if any)
3. For the good of the Order[2]
4. Closing

OPENING

EA: *After Astral Temple has been built, all should leave the Temple except for EA.*

H-r: *Opens portal and returns to the first station, facing North if the Portal is in the South-West [or South if the Portal is in the North-West], with staff uplifted at 45° angle and lamp held at heart.*

EA: * * * Fellow Initiates, take your stations and places.

All: *Members and officers enter in the order described above, passing the Portal with the Neophyte Signs and Password, and go directly to their stations or seats, where they remain standing.*

H-r: *Takes the Word for the current semester from each initiate as they enter, being prepared to block anyone who does not have the Word with the staff.*

No one is to gain admission without this Word. If word is forgotten, H-r says: "Very Honored, EA, the Word for the Semester has been lost." The EA then asks who seeks admission and if anyone can vouch for the stranger wishing entry. If yes, then the word is given by the one vouching upon the agreement of the EA.

H-r: When all are at places, close the portal and return to station.

EA: Be seated.

All: *Sit.*

EA directs a member to perform the Lesser Banishing Ritual of the Pentagram.

EA: (Frater/Soror) _____, please perform the Lesser Banishing Pentagram of Earth.

ORATION

EA: * * *

All: *Rise and face East.*

EA turns with the Sun to face East. Raises scepter aloft.

Officers elevate implements.

EA: Hidden Forces of that Limitless Light which establishes the boundaries of the Universe, we invoke ye by the all-powerful Name of your Creator (*pause*) to seal in just orientation the inner limits of this Temple. May the secret virtue of the radiant East be conferred this day upon the throne of the Adept of this Temple, who is the emblem of that Dawning Light which shall illuminate the paths of the unknown and shall guide us to the attainment of the Quintessence, the Stone of the Wise, perfect Wisdom and true Happiness.

All: So may it be! *Turn and face as usual.*

EA *Sits.*

All: S*it.*

CRY OF THE WATCHER

EA: * * *

H-r: Rises, carrying staff vertically, grasping it by the center in the right hand, white end uppermost. Leaves lamp at station and go by North to North East. Salutes EA by raising staff perpendicularly thrice. EA, sitting, acknowledges the salute, charging each of the three sections of the Staff, white, red, then black. H-r turns with Sun to face South-West, holds staff at an angle of 45° aloft, and says with FORCE:

H-r: Hence, hence, ye profane!

H-r returns to the station through the North, faces east, and remains standing.

FIRST DUTY

EA: (Frater/Soror) H-r.

H-r: Very Honored, EA.

EA: The first duty of Initiates?

H-r: To guard the Temple against the approach of the profane.

EA: Fulfill that duty.

H-r: *Opens the door, and if there be no Sentinel, fastens door of antechamber. If a Sentinel is in the antechamber, H-r merely ensures the sentinel's presence, returns to Temple and closes the door. Places the lamp before the door. Taking staff by the white end, H-r knocks on the floor with the black end * * *, then takes staff by the center and holds it aloft while pointing with his left hand to the Lantern and says:*

H-r: Very Honored, EA, the Temple is properly guarded.

EA: How guarded?

H-r: By the Staff of Science to bar the profane, and the Lamp of Wisdom to light the path of all true Initiates. (*Sits.*)

THE PASSWORD

EA: Honored A-n, have you the Word?

A-n: (*Rises and salutes EA with the sword.*)
I have, Very Honored EA.

EA: Then you will receive it from the C-n and P-r, who will assure themselves that all present possess it and communicate it to me.

A-n: Let the C-n and P-r approach the West.

C-n/P-r:

> *Go diagonally from their stations to the West of the altar, where they meet, and go together to a position before the A-n's throne, facing A-n. Together they give the Sign of Respect.*

A-n: *Returns Sign.*

A-n: (Frater/Soror) C-n, give me the Word. (*Done.*)
(Frater/Soror) P-r, give me the Word. (*Done.*)

A-n: The Word is true in the West. Assure yourselves that all present possess it. (*Sits.*)

C-n/P-r:

> *Proceed east, along their respective sides of the Temple, taking the Word from each person present. When they reach their stations, North and South, they go to the center to A-t, who receives the Word from C-n and communicates it to P-r. The two then wait at the West of the Pillars, facing East, C-n behind the white pillar and P-r behind the black pillar.*

A-t: *Rises, faces east and salutes with the scepter.*

Very Honored EA, the Word is true at the center.

Faces West and sits.

C-n/P-r:

Continue east along their respective sides of the Temple, receiving the Word as before. On the dais, C-n takes the Word from Steward., Pr-l, Sr. 2nd Order and PA. P-r receives it from C-s, Jr. 2nd Order and I-r. Both move before the EA and give the Sign of Respect, which the EA returns with the scepter.

C-n: Very Honored, EA, we bear the Word-
P-r: - from the West -
C-n: - through the Center -
P-r: - to the East.

EA: Communicate it to me.
C-n: *Gives EA the Word.*
P-r: *Gives EA the Word.*

EA: The Word is true in the East. Return to your stations.

C-n/P-r: *Salute, then return to their stations and sit.*

SIGNS

EA: *After a short pause, knocks * and rises.*

All: *All rise.*

EA: Affiliates of the vehicle of the Inner School, which is called (*name of organization*)_____, assist me to open _____ Lodge, Number ___, as a Hall of Neophytes. Honored A-n, assure yourself that all present have looked upon the Dawn.

A-n: Fratres et Sorores of (*name of organization*) _____, give the signs of Neophyte.

All give Signs toward the A-n, led by the A-t.[3]

A-n: Very Honored, EA.

(*A-n gives sign; EA echoes sign*),

all present have witnessed the Dawn.

SECRET NAME [4]

EA: The letters of our secret name:

EA: _
A-n: _
A-t: _

EA: ... they are also a veil for the Wheel of the Law.

ANTIPHONY[5]

EA	A-n
Alpha	O
First	L
Beginning	E

A-t: And the path of the W_ _ _ between.

EA	A-n
Dawn	T
Idea	F
Radiance	E

A-t: And the path of the L _ _ _ _ between.

EA	A-n
Youth	A
Increase	D
Forethought	A

A-t: And the path of H_ _ _ _ _ _ between.

STATIONS & DUTIES OF OFFICERS

EA: Officers, remain standing.

All: *All sit with EA, except officers.*

EA: Let the number of Officers in this grade, and the nature of their Offices be proclaimed once again, that the Powers whose images they are may be established in the spheres of those present and in the sphere of this Temple; for by Names and Images are all Powers awakened and reawakened.

Honored A-n, how many chief officers are there in this grade?

A-n: (*Salutes with Sword.*) Three, Very Honored EA, namely: A., A-n, and A-t.

EA: Is there any peculiarity in these names?

A-n: They all begin with the letter A.

EA: Of what is this letter a symbol?

A-n: Of life, as the source of all manifestation, for A is our equivalent for the Hebrew Aleph, symbol of the Life-Breath and sign of the Fiery Intelligence, which IS before all beginnings, which IS throughout all activities, which IS eternally, when all activity subsides into the still calm of Pure Being.

EA: How many assistant officers are there in this grade?

A-n: Three, namely: P-r, C-n and H-r.

EA: The station of the P-r?

A-n: In the North, Very Honored EA, to symbolize Cold and Moisture. (*Sits.*)

EA: (Frater/Soror) P-r, your duties?

P-r: (*Salutes*) I have charge of the robes and insignia of the officers.
I attend to the cup of purification.
I bear the Word from West to East, through the North.
I guard the Gate of the North,
and I am charged with the purification, by Water, of the Temple, of the Initiates, and of the candidate.

EA: The station of the C-n?

P-r: In the South, Very Honored EA to symbolize Heat and Dryness. (*Sits.*)

EA: (Frater/Soror) C-n, your duties?

C-n: (*Salutes*) I attend to the censer and the incense.
I bear the Word from West to East, through the South.
I guard the Gate of the South
, and I am charged with the consecration, with Fire, of the Temple, of the Initiates, and of the candidate.

EA: The station of the H-r?

C-n: Within the Portal, Very Honored EA. (*Sits.*)

EA: (Frater/Soror) H-r, your duties?

H-r: (*Salutes*)
I see that all furniture of the Temple is properly arranged before the Opening.
I guard the Portal.
I admit the Fratres et Sorores of this Order.
I assist in the reception of the candidate.
I attend to the lamp of my office.
I lead all circumambulations and processions.
I make all announcements and reports.

EA: What do your lamp and staff symbolize?

H-r: The light of occult science and directing power.

EA: The station of the A-t?

H-r: At the center of the Temple, facing the altar of the universe. (*Sits.*)

EA: (Frater/Soror) A-t, your duties?

A-t: *Turns with the Sun to face east. Salutes EA with scepter held at an angle of 45° and says:*

> I preside over the symbolic gateway of occult science.
> I am the reconciler between the light and the darkness.
> I immediately follow the H-r in the circumambulation.
> I superintend the candidate's preparation, lead him through the path of darkness into light, and assist at the reception, and I aid the other chief officers in the execution of their duties.

EA: What does the whiteness of your mantle symbolize?

A-t: Purity.

EA: Your ensign of office?

A-t: The Scepter of Equilibration.

EA: What does it symbolize?

A-t: The symmetry and balance of universal forces upon which we must depend for the execution of our plans.

EA: And what your office?

A-t: The pure quest for the light of truth, which should guide all human endeavors.

EA: The station of the A-n?

A-t: On the Throne of the West. (*Faces West & sits.*)

EA: Honored A-n, what does the Throne of the West symbolize?

A-n: (*Rises*) Increase of darkness and decrease of light.

EA: Your duties?

A-n: I preside over the twilight and darkness which encompass us in the absence of the Sun of life and light.
I guard the Gate of the West.
I assist in the reception of the candidate;
and I superintend the subordinate officers in the execution of their duties.

EA: What does the black color of your mantle symbolize?

A-n: Darkness.

EA: Your ensign of office?

A-n: The sword.

EA: What does the sword symbolize?

A-n: Severity and Judgment.

EA: And what your office?

A-n: Fortitude.

EA: The A.'s station?

A-n: On the throne of the East -

EA: * * *

All: (*Rise, except EA and Chiefs.*)

A-n: - which symbolizes the rising (*EA rises*) of the Sun of life and light. (His/Her) duty is to rule and govern this Lodge in accordance with the rules of the Order. The red color of (his/her) mantle symbolizes life. (His/Her) ensign is the Scepter of Dominion; and (his/her) office is that of Expounder of the Mysteries.

C-s: (*Rises*) My place is northeast of the EA. My duty is to observe the proceedings of this Lodge, record all things proper to be written, and be the custodian of all documents and properties. My yellow mantle symbolizes the Transparent Intelligence, penetrating all veils of ignorance. My ensign, the Scepter of Reconciliation, signifies the balance of opposites in the operation of the Great Work; and my office is that of witness to the Work of L.V.X.

I-r: (*Rises*) My place is East of the EA. My duty is to see to the Lodge's administration, make all appointments, receive all moneys, and make all proper payments. My red mantle symbolizes the Fiery Intelligence, which veils the causes with the Fire of Spirit. My ensign, the Scepter of the Pentalpha, symbolizes the ruling power of Spirit in all things; and my office is that of witness to the Work of L.V.X.

Pr-l: (*Rises*) My place is southeast of the EA. My duty is to supervise the ritual of this Lodge and to be the living voice transmitting the messages of its invisible Foundation. My blue mantle symbolizes the Uniting Intelligence which links all human hearts. My ensign, the Scepter of Unity, signifies the all-embracing power of sympathy; my office is witness to the Work of L.V.X.

PURIFICATION

EA: (Frater/Soror) P-r, I command you to purify the Temple and the Initiates by Water.

All: *All sit except P-r, who proceeds to carry out the command as follows:*

P-r: *Advances diagonally from station to East of Temple, before the throne of EA, carrying the cup in both hands. Facing EA, P-r gives Sign of Respect, to which EA responds as usual. P-r then holds the cup at the heart center and says:*

P-r:	I purify by Water.

Dips right thumb, forefinger, and middle finger held together in the cup of Water and sprinkles three times toward the East to form the points of a water triangle thus:

        1   2

          3

P-r then turns in place to face the station of the C-n in the South and says:

    I purify by Water.

P-r sprinkles again, then faces West and say:

    I purify by Water.

Sprinkles again, then faces own station in the North and says:

    I purify by Water.

Sprinkles a fourth time, then faces east again, gives the Sign of Respect, turns with the Sun to face their station, and walks there directly. At the station, places the cup on the pedestal, faces the EA and says:

P-r: The Temple is cleansed.

Remains standing at station, facing south, during the consecration.

CONSECRATION

C-n: *During the purification, prepare the censer with fresh incense. The censer should be actively smoking.*

EA: (Frater/Soror) C-n, I command you to consecrate the Temple and the Initiates with Fire.

C-n: *Advances diagonally from station to East of Temple, before the throne of EA, carrying censer in both hands. Facing East, C-n gives the Sign of Respect, to which the EA responds. Holding the censer at heart level, C-n says:*

C-n: I consecrate with Fire.

C-n: *Censes with three thrusts towards the East to form the points of a fire triangle, thus:*

```
            1

        2       3
```

C-n then turns in place to face their station in the South and says:
                    I consecrate with Fire.

C-n censes again in the same way, then faces West and says:
                    I consecrate with Fire.

Censes, faces the P-r's station in the North and says:
                    I consecrate with Fire.

Censes a fourth time, then faces east again, give the Sign of Respect, turns with the Sun to face their station, and walks there directly. At the station, places the censer on the pedestal, faces the EA, and says:

C-n: The Temple is consecrated.

Remains standing at station, facing North.

MYSTIC CIRCUMAMBULATION

EA: Rises, holding the scepter in the right hand. EA, P-r, and C-n thus formulate the White Triangle.

EA: Let the mystic circumambulation take place in the Path of Light.

All: At the word, "Light," all members rise and form the procession in the North.

Formation with Members in All Grades[6]

When the whole procession is in motion, it is in the following order: H-r, A-t, I-r, C-s, PA, 2nd Order Members, A-n, 0=0, P-r, 1=10, 2=9, C-n, 3=8, Jr. 4=7, Sr. 4=7.

Circumambulation Instruction

Pr-l: Remains seated and does not circle, but before the procession moves, may leave the station to verify that all are in the correct position. If Pr-l leaves station, EA waits until Pr-l has returned before signaling the procession to move.

EA: * Knocks once to begin procession as soon as A-n is in position and knocks each time the H-r passes East so that counting the knock, which signals the procession to move, the EA gives four knocks during the circumambulation. Except when giving the knocks of the four-fold battery, EA holds the scepter in his/her right hand, the arm fully extended with the point of the pentagram directed toward the West. The EA needs to formulate the intention of projecting light through the scepter and out from the point of the pentagram.

All: *No music is permissible during the circumambulation. Officers lower insignia, pointing horizontally in the direction they are moving, and members give the Sign of Projected Light as they pass the EA's extended scepter... [Description of sign and visualization deleted]*

A-n, A-t, C-n, and P-r, as they pass the EA, should formulate the intention, as they lower their insignia, of receiving the current of energy projected from the EA's scepter.

H-r: In passing east the first time, should formulate the intention of charging the white end of the staff. At the second passing, should think of the red portion as receiving the current. The third should intend the current to charge the black segment of the staff.

A-n: After passing the EA once, continues with the procession until arriving at A-n's throne, then leaves the procession and remains standing, facing east, holding the sword extended upward at an angle of 45°.

A-t: After passing EA the second time, continues with the procession until reaching the C-n's station, then leaves the procession and goes directly to A-t's station, standing facing West, holding the scepter at a 45° angle.

All: When the H-r and other officers and members have passed the EA three times, they continue around the Temple until they arrive at their proper stations and places. There they remain standing, facing as they usually do when seated.

After this circumambulation in the Opening and until the reverse circumambulation in the Closing, all passage in the Temple, whether the Lodge is in working session or in recess, must be in the direction of the established current, i.e., with the Sun. This permits direct crossing from North to South, or from South to North at any point. The current must be followed in movements from West to East or East to West.

EA: When officers and members have arrived at accustomed stations and places:

The mystic circumambulation is accomplished. It is symbolic of the rising light.

EA: Waits until the designated member goes to the light switch, switches on the light, and returns.

EA then continues:

ADORATION

EA: Let us adore the Lord of the Universe.

All: *All face east. EA signals to begin by holding the scepter aloft, arm fully extended at a 45° angle. As Adoration begins, EA returns the scepter to its usual position. A-n and A-t similarly extend their implements at a 45° angle. H-r holds the staff upright and vertically, white end upward so that H-r's forearm is in the same posture as EA's scepter. C-n and P-r hold their implements at heart level. After each line, officers lower insignia; members make the Sign of Projected Light. After the "Amen," all give the Sign of Silence.*

> Holy art Thou, Lord of the Universe.
> (*Sign of Projected Light*)
>
> Holy art Thou, whom Nature hath not formed.
> (*Sign of Projected Light*)
>
> Holy art Thou, the Vast and the Mighty One.
> (*Sign of Projected Light*)
>
> Lord of the Light and of the Darkness.
> (*Sign of Projected Light*)

Amen.   (*Sign of Silence*)

All face as usual, and remain standing.

DECLARATION

EA: (Frater/Soror) H-r, in the name of the Lord of the Universe, I command you to declare that I have opened _____ Lodge, No. __ as a Hall of Neophytes.

EA: *
A-n: *
A-t: *

H-r: *Leaves lamp at station, advances to the northeast before the dais, faces EA holding the staff in the left hand by the center, white end upward, and gives the Sign of Respect; then transfers staff to the right hand and, grasping it by the center, faces West; raises arm to 45° angle and holds staff perpendicularly; says:*

In the name of the Lord of the Universe, I declare that the Sun has arisen, and that the Light shineth in the Darkness.

Lowers staff and, following the current, returns to station and remains standing.

MYSTIC WORDS

EA:	Khabs.	*
A-n:	Am.	*
A-t:	Pekht.	*
A-n:	Konx.	*
A-t:	Om.	*
EA:	Pax.	*
A-t:	Light.	*
EA:	In.	*
A-n:	Extension.	*

SIGNS

EA: Fratres et Sorores, the signs.

All: *Members and officers give both signs toward the altar, following A-t.*

EA *sits.*

All *sit.*

ADMISSION OF LATECOMERS [7]

RECESS

After any latecomers and visitors have taken their places, the EA can call a Recess.

EA: ** I now declare a suspension of the work in this Lodge until the Initiates are recalled to their stations and places by the H-r.

All: *Mantles of officers and lamens are left at their stations during recess. Aprons and baldricks may be worn during recess, but only in the antechamber. All members and officers must remove their apron and baldric before leaving the antechamber.*

END OF OPENING

CLOSING

EA: *When the EA desires to resume work, he/she informs the H-r*

H-r: *Goes to the antechamber, stands in the Portal, knocks sharply on the floor with the black end of the staff, holding it by the white end, and says:*

* * * Fellow Initiates, the EA calls the Lodge to resume work. Repair to your accustomed stations and places, and clothe yourselves for labor.

At the door, take note as each enters so that none may enter the Temple without being correctly clothed for labor or giving the proper signs.

All: *Enter in any sequence. All must make the two signs on entering the Temple and wear proper aprons and baldricks.*

All sit.

EA: *When members and officers, clothed for work, are seated at their proper stations and places:*

* * * (*All Rise*) Affiliates of that vehicle of the Inner School, which is called the (name of organization) _____, assist me to close _____ Lodge, No._____ as a Hall of Neophytes.

(Frater/Soror) H-r, see that the Temple is properly guarded.

H-r: *Proceeds as in Opening and knocks on the floor with the black end of the staff, holding it by the white end:* * * *.

Very Honored EA, the Temple is properly guarded.

THE SIGNS

EA: Honored A-n, assure yourself that all present have looked upon the Dawn.

A-n: Fratres et Sorores of the (name of organization)_____, give the signs of a Neophyte.

All: *All except EA and A-n give signs, following the lead of A-t.*

A-n: Very Honored EA (*Places sword on the pedestal and gives signs toward East. EA returns signs*), all present have seen the Light.

EA *sits.*

All *sit.*

PURIFICATION AND CONSECRATION

EA: (Frater/Soror) P-r, I command you to purify the Temple and the Initiates by Water.

P-r: *Goes with the Sun to a position facing EA, salutes, and purifies as in the Opening. When P-r has faced EA after the fourth purification, he/she salutes and returns by way of the Sun until reaching the station of C-n. Then, he/she crosses between the A-t and the altar to own station and completes the ceremony as in the Opening:*

P-r: The Temple is cleansed.

(*Remains standing during the consecration.*)

EA: (Frater/Soror) C-n, I command you to consecrate the Temple and the Initiates with Fire.

C-n: *Crosses Temple between the A-t and the altar, to North, goes with the Sun to station of EA, and salutes. C-n then performs the consecration as in the Opening. When C-n has saluted EA the second time, he/she returns to own station with the Sun. Puts the censer on the pedestal and says:*

C-n: The Temple is consecrated.

P-r/C-n: (*Sit.*)

LIGHT AND SOUND

(Sound and Color)[8]

EA: Let the forces of Light and of Sound be directed by us... [omitted text]

All: *Cantor goes to place in the southeast.*

CHART 1

A-n: *Displays the Color Chart 1: Red, Yellow, Blue-green.*

EA: May the Fire of the Ram... [omitted text] ...bring life and light to all creatures.

All: *Cantor sounds the tones C, E, and G. As each note is sounded, the members who are to intone it hum it softly. They who intone C look at the Red panel. They who intone E look at the Yellow panel. They who intone G look at the Blue-green panel. All then intone thrice:*

I A O (pronounced "ee-ah-oh")

CHART 2

A-n: *Holds up Chart 2: Red-orange, Yellow-green, Blue.*

A-n: May the fertile Earth of the Bull... [omitted text] ...bring life and light to all creatures.

All: *Cantor sounds tones C-sharp, F, and G-sharp, corresponding, respectively, to Red-orange, Yellow-green, and Blue. Notes hummed as before. All then intone thrice:*

I A O

CHART 3

A-n: *Holds up Chart 3: Orange, Green, Blue-violet.*

A-t: May the breath of the Lovers... [omitted text] ...bring life and light to all creatures.

All: *Cantor sounds tones D, F-sharp, and A, corresponding, respectively, to Orange, Green, and Blue-violet. Notes hummed as before. All then intone thrice:*

I A O

CHART 4

A-n: *Holds up Chart 4: Yellow-orange, Blue-green, Violet.*

C-n: *May the streams of Celestial... [omitted text] ...bring life and light to all creatures.*

All: *Cantor sounds tones D-sharp, G, and A-sharp, corresponding, respectively, to Yellow-orange, Blue-green, and Violet. Notes hummed as before. All then intone thrice:*

I A O

CHART 5

A-n: *Holds up Chart 5: Yellow, Blue, Red-violet.*

P-r: *May the strength of Pure Hearts... [omitted text] ...bring life and light to all creatures.*

All: *Cantor sounds tones E, G-sharp, and B, corresponding, respectively, to Yellow, Blue and Red-violet. Notes hummed as before. All then intone thrice:*

I A O

Cantor returns to seat.

REVERSE CIRCUMAMBULATION

EA: Let the Mystic Reverse Circumambulation take place in the path of Light.

All: *Done as in Opening, except that procession forms in the South by the station of the C-n, and the order of procession is: H-r, A-t, I-r, C-s, PA, 2nd Order members, A-n, Senior 4=7, Junior 4=7, 3=8, C-n, 2=9, 1=10, P-r, 0=0, newest initiate (s) last. The procession moves around the Temple in reverse direction, crossing the East from South to North. A-n and A-t leave the procession as in the Opening, except that A-t goes from the station of P-r to their station at the second round. All others pass the East three times. Because this circumambulation aims to break the current, the entire procession should form before it begins to move.*

EA: When the procession is formed, EA starts circumambulation with one knock *, and knocks once * each time the H-r passes the east. Officers lower their insignia, and members give the Sign of Projected Light as they pass EA. When all have returned to their proper stations and places, EA says:

EA: The mystic reverse circumambulation is accomplished. It is symbolic of the fading light.

When the Temple is provided with dimming lights, they should be lowered as the procession moves. Otherwise, lights should be dimmed/extinguished when the EA says, "fading light." This requires that all subsequent speeches be memorized.

ADORATION

EA: Let us adore the Lord of the Universe. (*Turns with the Sun to the East.*)

All: *Turn with the Sun to face east. EA faces east, raising the scepter to signal the start of the Adoration. Words and gestures in Adoration are the same in Opening. After Adoration, all face as usual.*

EA sits.

All sit.

MYSTIC REPAST

EA: Nothing now remains but in silence together to partake of the Mystic Repast, composed of the symbols of the four elements, and to remember our pledge of secrecy.

H-r: *Goes to P-r's station, takes the cup and places it at the west side of the altar, moving the triangle and cross toward the altar center to make room for the base of the cup. Sees the rose, bread, salt, and red lamp are correctly arranged. Returns to station and sits.*

> EA: *Hands Scepter to PA or places scepter on the pedestal, goes down the center of Lodge, passing between the white pillar and A-t, and passing altar on the south side. EA faces east at the West of the altar, gives both signs and comes close to the altar, crossing arms over the breast.*

EA: I invite you to inhale with me the perfume of this rose, a symbol of air.

Elevates rose, inhales its perfume, and replaces rose.

To feel with me the flame of this sacred Fire.

Elevates the red lamp and then replaces it; holds hands over the lamp, palms down.

To eat with me this Bread and Salt as types of Earth.

Elevates the paten and replaces it, then takes bread dipped in salt.

And finally, to share with me the purification of this consecrated cup of elemental Water.

Puts bread in mouth, elevates cup, replaces it on the altar, dips right forefinger in the cup and signs himself/herself on the forehead with the points of a water triangle, thus:

right eyebrow	left eyebrow
1	2
root of nose	
3	

All: *All receive in turn singly, each from his or her predecessor, who goes East of the altar to administer. Each person who receives the elements makes the two signs of the Grade west of the altar before receiving the rose. Only the EA elevates any elements or signs on his/her forehead. The member giving the elements stands East of the altar to give the rose, passes South of the altar to lift the red lamp and replace it, then passes East of the altar to its north side to give bread and salt and make the sign of purification.*

As each element is used, it is replaced carefully in its proper position on the altar. All sacraments are offered over the cup. THE CUP IS NOT LIFTED FROM ITS PLACE.

After giving the sign of purification, the member who gives it goes to his/her station or place in the Temple by the most direct route from the north side of the altar.

The order of precedence is EA; Pr-l; I-r; C-s; PA; 2nd Order members; A-n, A-t, C-n, P-r, Sr. 4=7 [Portal], Jr. 4=7, 3=8; 2=9, 1=10; and 0=0.

When H-r has received the sign of purification, the member who has given it returns to his/her place.

H-r: *Takes cup to P-r's station; faces East; elevates the cup; places cup on P-r's pedestal, and says:*

> It is finished.

Returns to station and sits.

MYSTIC WORDS

EA:	Khabs.	*
A-n:	Am.	*
A-t:	Pekht.	*
A-n:	Konx.	*
A-t:	Om.	*
EA:	Pax.	*
A-t:	Light.	*
EA:	In.	*
A-n:	Extension.	*

EA: (*Seated.*) May this symbolic sacrament sustain us in our search for the Quintessence, the Stone of the Wise, Happiness, Wisdom, and the Highest Good!

DECLARATION

EA: I now declare Lodge, No. _____ closed as a Hall of Neophytes.

EA: *
A-n: *
A-t: *

CHAPTER 1 NOTES

[1] מתחיל *mat.cheel.* Beginner, novice, greenhorn.

[2] For the good of the Order.

Usually, after the opening, there is a break, and the members meet in the Temple where announcements are made, lodge business, and then a talk is given by the EA.

Personally, I find this activity breaks up the magical energy. I prefer a short break after the opening to get a drink of water or a quick bite to eat. Low blood sugar and ritual work do not go well together. Then, begin the closing ritual. After the temple labor is completed, have a talk and lodge business.

[3] Do not hurry the step and signs. It should be done with rhythm. The step is one count, then raise the arms for count 2, visualize for count 3, lower the arms for count 4 and the sign of silence for the last count.

[4] The letters are omitted.

[5] The first letter of each word is given for the A-n part.

[6] Formation with Members in All Grades

Creating a flowing start to the mystic circumambulation requires practice and changes when members advance through the grades. In addition, it is confusing, so we usually line up by the P-r station and wait for the EA's knock to start the procession.

[7] ADMISSION OF LATECOMERS

Members arriving late rarely happens, so I moved this section of the ritual to keep the flow of the Opening Ritual.

When there is no Sentinel, the EA must declare a recess after the Opening so that the antechamber door, which must always be locked in the absence of a Sentinel, may be opened to permit latecomers or visitors to be tested. Otherwise, the recess is at the pleasure of the EA. In any case, the formula for the recess is not to be used until all latecomers and visitors have taken their proper places. The Formula for Recess is:

Without Sentinel

[A sentinel is a member who sits outside and ensures no one enters the Temple during the ritual. However, members don't like sitting outside and missing the ceremony. We never had anyone try to enter the ritual space, so the position was eliminated, and the H-r performs the duties of the sentinel.]

H-r: *Goes to the antechamber and assures himself that anyone waiting has the Word. Having done this, H-r returns to the Temple, faces east, and raises the staff in salute, saying:*

H-r: Very Honored EA, an Initiate (or a group of Initiates) desire(s) admission.

EA: (Has/Have) (she/he/they) the Password for the present time?

H-r: (She/He/They) (has/have.)

EA: Permit (her/him/them) to enter.

H-r: Opens door. Waiting member(s) now enter. Those admitted go to the West of the altar and face east. They give the Sign of Respect, followed by the signs of the grade. EA, standing, answers those signs. The members then repair to their places in the Temple, following the course of the Sun.

[8] SOUND AND COLOR

For more information on sound and color attunement, see *Healing with Sound and Vibrational Attunement* by Kevin Townley

CHAPTER 2

CEREMONY OF ADMISSION

Before the initiation, the Opening Ceremony is performed. Then a short break to ensure the kneeler, blindfold and other items are nearby. The temple is ready once the EA is satisfied, and the Ceremony of Admission begins.

The structure of the PFC ritual is the same as the Golden Dawn.

ADMISSION CEREMONY SECTIONS

CROSSING THE PORTAL

1st PURIFICATION AND CONSECRATION

OBLIGATION

PASSING OF THE GATES

1st CIRCUMAMBULATION

2nd CIRCUMAMBULATION

2nd PURIFICATION AND CONSECRATION

3rd, PURIFICATION AND CONSECRATION

3rd CIRCUMAMBULATION

INVOCATION

SECRET NAME

ANTIPHONY

THE MYSTIC WORDS

H-r's LAMP

SIGNS, GRIP AND PASSWORD(S)

BETWEEN THE PILLARS

FINAL PURIFICATION AND CONSECRATION

INVESTITURE

EA LECTURE

PROCLAMATION

A-n's ADDRESS

EA's FINAL INSTRUCTION

ASPIRATION NAME

RECESS
    END OF ADMISSION CEREMONY

CLOSING

Similarities Between the PFC and GD Rituals

1. The OBLIGATION is similar, but there are significant differences.

2. The two rituals are almost identical, from the PASSING OF THE GATES to the INVOCATION. The main difference is the addition of chanting in the PFC ritual.

3. The MYSTIC WORDS and H-r's LAMP section are the same.

4. The EA LECTURE is similar in both rituals.

5. The PROCLAMATION is the same.

6. The A-n's ADDRESS in the two rituals is almost identical.

Differences Between the Rituals

1. PFC ritual questions of the candidate before entering the temple. This is not done in the GD ritual.

2. The SECRET NAME and ANTIPHONY are unique to the PFC ritual.

3. The INVESTITURE lecture is different because the PFC ritual has an apron with symbols that need explanation.

4. The Sign of Projected Light differs from the GD Saluting Sign. Also, the grip and password are different.

5. After the A-n's ADDRESS, the Golden Dawn Ritual is complete. The PFC ritual has the new initiate choose an ASPIRATION NAME.

CEREMONY OF ADMISSION

HEBREW NAME: שער הפרס חכמה [1]

Before the Opening, one of the Lodge members unknown to the candidate is designated to act as Stranger to guide the candidate. After the Opening, the Stranger leaves the Temple and dresses in black. This may consist of donning a black robe over the white robe or changing into other black clothes. The Stranger also carries or wears a red rose as an identification mark.

The Stranger goes to the candidate waiting outside the building and bearing a red rose. Asking the candidate to follow silently, the Stranger takes the candidate to the antechamber, asks for the candidate's rose, and instructs him/her to wait there. The Stranger leaves the candidate, closes the door, then revests in Temple attire. Carrying the rose, the Stranger enters the Temple, goes to the altar, places the rose next to the altar rose, returns to his/her own station or place, and sits.

EA: * Fratres et Sorores of ____ Lodge No.____ of the (*name of organization*)_____, your Chiefs have considered the application of _____ for admission to this Order and have passed favorably thereon.

(Frater/Soror) P-r, assure yourself that the candidate begins this undertaking with the proper understanding of its nature.

(Frater/Soror) A-t, instruct the candidate to hold (him/herself) in readiness for the ceremony of (his/her) admission and superintend (his/her) preparation.

A-t/P-r:

> *Rise together, bearing their insignia, face EA, and salute. They go to Candidate, the P-r preceding the A-t, following the solar course from their stations to the southwest portal.*

C-n: *Removes A-t's chair and pedestal from between the Pillars to a place immediately east of C-n's station.*

H-r: *Moves chair and scepter stand away from the portal to allow as much room as possible for the floor officers to maneuver around the blindfolded candidate.*

H-r: *Ensures that a hassock is ready at the West of the altar for the candidate to kneel on.*

P-r: *(In antechamber)* (Candidate's name),_____ I am instructed to ask you if you enter upon this undertaking of your own accord, prompted only by a desire for enlightenment and the hope of becoming of greater service to humanity; mindful of the seriousness of your decision; and intending to conform cheerfully to the usages of our Fraternity. Do you so approach our portal?

CAN: I do.

P-r: *Returns to station, entering Temple by northwest portal if there be one, faces EA, salutes with Sign of Respect, and says:*

Very Honored, EA.

EA: (Frater/Soror) P-r.

P-r: The Candidate has signified (his/her) understanding of the undertaking (he/she) is now about to enter and (his/her) intention to conform cheerfully to the usages and rules of our Order. *(Sits)*

A-t: *After P-r returns to Temple, A-t superintends the candidate's preparation. First, the candidate is hoodwinked, then clad in a white robe, with a black robe as an outer garment. Next, a rope is wound three times around the waist and tied. Thus prepared, the candidate is led by A-t to the door of Temple, the northwest portal if there be one. A-t, who may have assistants if there is more than one candidate, takes the candidate's right hand in their left hand for leading. As they approach the portal, A-t says:*

A-t: Child of Earth, arise and enter the Path of Darkness.

(Knocks * * * on the outer side of the door with the butt of the scepter.)

H-r: Very Honored, EA. There is an alarm at the portal.

EA: Ascertain what it is and report to me.

H-r: *Takes lamp, which is retained during the entire initiation, opens the door and says:*

Who comes here?

A-t: A Child of Earth, risen from the grave of error, seeking Light at the end of the Path of Darkness.

H-r: Does (he/she) come of (his/her) own accord?

A-t: (He/she) does.

H-r: Has (he/she) been duly reminded of the seriousness of (his/her) undertaking?

A-t: (He/she) has.

H-r: Then let (him/her) wait until I have informed the EA and the Lodge. *(Closes door and faces EA).* Very Honored EA, Fratres et Sorores, there awaits a Child of Earth at the portal, risen from the grave of error and seeking Light at the end of the Path of Darkness.

EA: Does (he/she) come of (his/her) own accord?

H-r: (He/she) does.

EA: Has (he/she) been duly reminded of the seriousness of (his/her) undertaking?

H-r: (He/she) has.

EA: Then let (him/her) enter the Path of Darkness in the Name of the Ineffable ONE. Let the C-n and P-r join in (his/her) reception.

CROSSING THE PORTAL

C-n/Pur:

> *C-n stands with the censer. P-r, with the cup, cross directly to the station of C-n, then both move together with the current to the portal.*

As they stand facing West, C-n is on P-r's left.

H-r: (*Opens door.*) It is the command of the EA that the candidate shall now enter the Path of Darkness in the Name of the Ineffable ONE.

A-t: *Leads candidate across the threshold and closes the door. If more than one candidate, they are placed side by side, close together, facing East.*

C-n: *Holds H-r's lamp until the conclusion of the following speech.*

H-r: *Stands in front of the candidate and bars the way with staff, one hand on the white section, the other on the black, held horizontally. Presses staff firmly against the candidate's chest so they can feel the obstacle.*

H-r: Child of Earth, unpurified and unconsecrated, thou mayest not enter here.

Removes staff from a horizontal position, steps back, and reclaims lamp from C-n.

1st PURIFICATION AND CONSECRATION

P-r: *Advances to Candidate, dips right forefinger in cup, and signs Can. as in Mystic Repast, saying:*

Child of Earth, I purify thee by water.
(Returns to former position.)

C-n: *Advances to Candidate, censes them with fire triangle as in consecrating the Temple, saying:*

Child of Earth, I consecrate thee with fire.
(Returns to former position.)

EA: Conduct the candidate to the foot of the altar.

A-t leads the candidate to the west side of the altar, facing East.

H-r follows and stands behind the candidate.

C-n stands right of H-r.

P-r stands left of H-r so that the C-n is now on the right side of the P-r.

EA: Child of Earth, whence came you, and why do you request admission into this Order?

CAN: *(Prompted by A-t)* From the darkness of the outer/ seeking the Light of occult knowledge in this Order/ where I believe this Light may be found.

EA: Why do you seek this knowledge?

CAN: *(Prompted)* I seek to know in order to serve.

EA: To whom do you offer your service?

CAN: *(Prompted)* To the One Source,/ that I may serve all Life./ To all Humanity,/ that the Empire of Light/ and the Reign of Harmony/ may be manifest here on Earth./ To my own Higher Self,/ that my service shall be guided by Truth.

EA: _____, you have signed a preliminary pledge to keep secret all relating to this Order. To confirm that pledge, you must now take a further obligation to keep inviolate the secrets and mysteries of this Order. After receiving my assurance that this obligation will bind you to nothing incompatible with your civil, moral, or religious duties, are you willing to take it?

CAN: <u>*(Not prompted)*</u> I am.

EA: *Leaves book and scepter on the throne. Advances through the Temple's center to the altar's east side.*

A-n: *Goes to the north side of the altar, drawn sword in right hand, and faces South.*

A-t: *With scepter, goes to the south side of the altar and faces North. The three Chief Officers form a Triangle.*

H-r: *Moves to the northeast corner of the altar, places lantern on the floor, and holds a staff in the left hand, leaving the right hand free to hold obligation while EA reads it.*

EA: Then, you will be assisted to kneel on both knees.

C-n/P-r:

Assists candidate to kneel. When Can. is on their knees, EA continues:

EA: Fellow Initiates, stand ye to witness this pledge.

All: *Rise and remain standing during obligation.*

EA: Give me your right hand, which I place on this symbol, sacred and sublime.

Places candidate's right hand, palm down, touching triangle. Next, place your left hand and palm upward on the back of the candidate's right hand.

EA: Place your left hand in mine.

Guides candidate's left hand with own right hand. If there be two candidates, the right hand of the second is placed palm down on the right hand of the first, the left hand of the first is taken by EA in the latter's left hand, and the left hand of the second is placed, palm down, on the left hand of first.

OBLIGATION

EA: Bow your head and say after me:

EA: I, (repeat your full name),/ in the presence of the Lord of the Universe/ and of this Lodge/ of Initiates of the (*name of organization*)_____,/ do, of my own accord,/ hereby and hereon,/ solemnly pledge myself/ to keep secret/ the esoteric name of this Order,/ the proceedings at its assemblies,/ its rites,/ signs,/ words and tokens,/ and every detail/ of its secret instruction,/ from every person in the world,/ except one duly initiated,/ whom I have tested and tried,/ so that I know him or her/ to be a true Initiate.

Furthermore, I will keep secret/ all information/ relative to the practical application of the secret instruction,/ and I also pledge myself/ to divulge nothing/ concerning the mysteries of the Order/ to the outside world,/ in the event of my resignation,/ demission,/ or expulsion therefrom.

I will devote my best efforts/ to promote fraternal harmony/ within this Order,/ and the welfare of humanity/ outside the Order also.

I will faithfully observe/ the regulations of the Order/ and of this Lodge/ as to the possession or circulation of aught/ relating to either or both;/ whether printed or written,/ delineated,/ carved or modeled;/ whether badge or ornament,/ symbol, picture or adjunct;/ and will return the same to the Order/ on due demand;/ whether lent to me,/ or purchased,/ or copied by me./ And in the event/ of my death or incapacity/ instructions will be left/ with my representatives/ to return the same unexamined.

I promise to undertake/ the serious study of occult knowledge,/ and to persevere/ through ceremonies and tests./ And whatever occult knowledge or power I may now have/ or may hereafter gain/ I will employ/ for naught but good.

All these points/ I, generally and severally/ upon this symbol sacred and sublime/ promise to observe,/ without evasion,/ equivocation,/ or mental reservation,/ under no less a penalty,/ should I knowingly and willfully/ violate any of them,/ than that of being expelled from this Order/ as a perjured liar/ unfit for the society/ of all upright and true persons;/ and, in addition,/ under the awful and just penalty/

A-n goes to a place behind the candidate.

> of having placed myself,/ by my unworthiness,/ in opposition to the current of that strong force/ of all forces,/ which is the power of life and growth/ to all who obey its law,/ and, to those who disobey it/ the instrument of death and destruction,/ smiting them/ as by lightning of heaven.

A-n: *Presses flat of sword-blade, guiding it carefully against the nape of candidate's neck, and immediately withdraws it. Returns to a position north of the altar, facing south.*

EA/CAN:

> So help me, the Lord of the Universe/ and my own Higher Soul.

All: So may it be.

All: *Sit except officers and assistants in the group at the altar.*

EA: *(Disengaging hands)* Rise, newly obligated Neophyte of the (*name of organization*)_____.

A-t: *Done. A-t assists the Neophyte in rising and turns him/her so he/she faces North.*

EA: Place the Neophyte[2] in the northern quarter of the Temple, the place of greatest symbolic darkness.

EA/A-n: *Return to their thrones and are seated.*

H-r: *With lamp and staff, advances North, next to the station of the P-r.*

A-t: *Escorts candidate to a position immediately behind H-r.*

P-r/C-n:

Follow the candidate, side by side, in the Procession, P-r behind the left side of Candidate & C-n behind and to the right.

PASSING OF THE GATES

EA: The Voice of my Higher Soul said unto me: "Let me enter the Path of Darkness. I am the only being in an abyss of Darkness. From the Darkness came I forth ere my birth; from the silence of a primal sleep."

And the Voice of Ages answered unto my soul: "I am the ONE who formulates in Darkness."

Child of Earth, the Light shineth in the Darkness, but the Darkness comprehends it not.

Let the mystic circumambulation take place in the Path of Darkness, with the symbolic lamp of occult wisdom to guide the way.

1st CIRCUMAMBULATION [3]

H-r: *The Procession moves, H-r leading, with lamp in the left hand and staff in the right. A-t guides the candidate, and the P-r and C-n follow, 3 times round, with the course of the Sun, reckoning from West of the altar.*

EA: * *(as they pass)*

All: *(Cantor sounds tone E. All intone the following, beginning after EA's knock:)*

My word shall go before thee/ As a pillar of fire by night/ And as a pillar of cloud/ Shalt thou follow it by day.[4]

A-n: * *(as they pass)*

2nd CIRCUMAMBULATION

EA: * *(as they pass)*

H-r: *When next reaching a point southeast of A-n's throne, turns, holding staff by the center, horizontally, with the right hand only. Presses staff against Neophyte's chest, as at reception.*

H-r: Child of Earth, unpurified and unconsecrated, thou canst not enter the Path of the West.

2nd PURIFICATION AND CONSECRATION

P-r: *(Signs Neophyte with water, as before.)*
Child of Earth, I purify thee by water.

C-n: *(Censes Neophyte as before.)*
Child of Earth, I consecrate thee with fire.

A-t: Child of Earth, twice purified and twice consecrated, thou mayest approach the gate of the West.

A-t: Procession moves to the West.

A-t: In the West, turns Neophyte to face A-n.

A-n: Rises and faces Neophyte, menacing him/her with the sword.

A-t: Raises hoodwink and then lowers it quickly so Neophyte can briefly see A-n.

A-n: Thou canst not pass by me, saith the Guardian of the West, unless thou canst tell me my name.

A-t: *(for Neophyte)* Darkness is thy name, the Great One of the Paths of Shades.

A-n: *(Slowly sinking point of the sword)* Fear is failure, Child of Earth, therefore be without fear, for in the heart of the coward virtue abide not. Thou hast known me, so pass thou on. *(Sits)*

(Procession continues.)

A-n: * *(as they pass)*

All: Cantor sounds tone G-sharp. All intone on that note the following:

> I am the Water of Life,/ the mute, dark mirror of substance,/ Reflecting Myself to Myself.

H-r: *Upon reaching the northeast, turns and bars the way as before, saying:*

Child of Earth, unpurified and unconsecrated, thou canst not enter the Path of the East.

3rd, PURIFICATION AND CONSECRATION

P-r: *(Signs Neophyte as before.)* Child of Earth, I purify thee by water.

C-n: *(Censes Neophyte as before.)* Child of Earth, I consecrate thee with fire.

A-t: Child of Earth, thrice purified, thrice consecrated, thou mayest approach the Gate of the East.

A-t: *Procession moves to the East. A-t turns Neophyte to face EA.*

EA: *Rises and faces Neophyte, menacing with the scepter.*

A-t: *Raises hoodwink and then lowers it quickly so Neophyte can briefly see EA.*

EA: Thou canst not pass by me, saith the Guardian of the East, unless thou canst tell me my name.

A-t: *(for Neophyte)* Light dawning in darkness is thy name, the Light of the Golden Day.

EA: Child of Earth, remember that unbalanced force is evil. Unbalanced Mercy is but weakness; unbalanced Severity but oppression. Thou has known me, so pass thou on, unto the Altar of the Universe. *(Sits.)*

(Procession moves on.)

3rd CIRCUMAMBULATION

EA: * *(as they pass)*

All: *Cantor sounds the tone C. All intone on that note the following:*

I am the circle of eternal flame, Self-fed./ From this Fire all things proceed,/ In it, all things have their being,/ And to it all return.

The procession arrives at the altar just as the word "return" is intoned.[5]

H-r/A-t: *Procession moves to the west side of the altar. Neophyte is turned to face East.*

A-n: *With Sword, goes North of the altar and faces South.*

P-r/C-n: *Stand behind Candidate, left and right, respectively.*

EA: *Leaves Throne, carrying the scepter, and stands between the Pillars, facing the candidate, then slowly advances toward the altar, saying:*[6]

EA: I come in the Power of the Light./
I come in the Light of Wisdom./
I come in the Mercy of the Light./
The Light hath Healing in its Wings.

INVOCATION

EA: *(At Altar)* Let the Neophyte be assisted to kneel.

A-t: *Assists Neophyte, then goes to the South of the altar and faces North.*

H-r: *At the same time, H-r goes North to the northeast corner of the altar, carrying lamp and staff, and faces southwest.*

EA/A-n/A-t:

Bring scepters and sword together over the altar so that the hexagram rests on the sword point, and the pentagram covers both.

EA: Fellow Initiates, stand with me to invoke the Lord of the Universe.

All: Rise.

EA: Lord of the Universe, the Vast One, the Mighty One, Ruler of the Light and of the Darkness. Thee we adore! Thee we invoke! Look with favor upon this Neophyte who kneels before Thee, and grant Thine aid unto the higher aspirations of (his/her) soul, so that (he/she) may prove a true and faithful (Frater/Soror) among us, to the glory of Thine Ineffable Name.

All: **Amen.**

EA/A-n/A-t:

> *Chief officers break the formation of their insignia over the altar.*

P-r/C-n

> *Advance to Neophyte and unfasten hoodwink, holding it ready for instant removal.*

EA: Let the Neophyte be assisted to rise.

C-n/P-r: *C-n and P-r assist, keeping the hoodwink in place as they do so.*

EA: Child of Earth, long hast thou dwelt in darkness. Quit the Night and seek the Day!

All: *At the word "day," hoodwink is suddenly removed, and all clap hands together sharply, once, taking timing from A-t.*

EA/A-n/A-t:

> *Standing at Altar as for Invocation, join points of insignia as before so that the union point is over Neophyte's head.*

EA: (Frater/Soror) __(name)__.

All: We receive thee into the company of Initiates of the (name of organization)_____.

EA/A-n/A-t: Take down their scepters and sword.

P-r/C-n: *Return to their stations with the Sun, & sit.*

All: *All sit except for EA, A-n, A-t, and H-r.*

SECRET NAME [7]

EA: Attend to the manifestation of our secret name.

EA: _
A-n: _
A-t: _

All: *Cantor sounds tone E., and all intone:*

— — —
ANTIPHONY [8]

EA	A-n
Alpha	O
First	L
Beginning	E

A-t: And the path of the W_ _ _ between.

EA	A-n
Dawn	T
Idea	F
Radiance	E

A-t: And the path of the L _ _ _ _ between.

EA	A-n
Youth	A
Increase	D
Forethought	A

A-t: And the path of H_ _ _ _ _ _ _ between.

THE MYSTIC WORDS

EA:	Khabs.	*
A-n:	Am.	*
A-t:	Pekht.	*

A-n:	Konx.	*
A-t:	Om.	*
EA:	Pax.	*

A-t:	Light.	*
EA:	In.	*
A-n:	Extension.	*

H-r's LAMP

EA: Let the H-r advance.

H-r: *Comes close to the northeast corner of the altar and holds lamp at breast height.*

EA: In all thy wanderings through darkness, the lamp of the H-r went before thee, though you saw it not. It symbolizes the light of occult wisdom, which the profane see not, neither do they know. (Pause.) Let the Neophyte be conducted to the East of the altar.

EA: *Returns to the throne, where he/she stands, facing West.*

A-t: *Conducts Neophyte from the North to the east side of the altar and tells Neophyte to remain there.*

H-r: *At the same time, moves north of the black pillar to a position between the Pillars, facing West.*

A-n: At the same time, goes, with the Sun, to position immediately west of the black pillar and stands there, facing West.

A-t: Goes between Neophyte and Altar, with the Sun, to the station of P-r, then crosses to the South, but East of Pillars, and takes position immediately west of the white pillar, facing West.

Thus, the three chief officers form a triangle; the three subordinate officers form a line from North to South; and the Neophyte stands facing the H-r, who is between the Pillars, and the EA, who is at his/her throne.

SIGNS, GRIP, AND PASSWORD

EA: *(After a brief pause)* Honored A-n, I delegate to you the office of entrusting the Neophyte with the secret signs, grip, word and present password of this Grade of the *(name of organization)*_____, and of superintending (his/her) fourth and final purification and consecration. *(Sits.)*

A-n: *Gives sword to P-r and advances to a position between Neophyte and H-r, facing Neophyte, who copies each sign, etc.*

A-n: (Frater/Soror)_____, I now proceed to instruct you in the step, secret signs, grip or token, and password of this Grade:

Advance your left foot about six inches. (Done.)
This is the Step of the Grade.
(Puts foot back.)

The signs are two: the Sign of Projected Light and the Sign of Silence. The first should always be answered by the second.

The Sign of Projected Light is given by advancing your left foot about six inches as in the step, and extending both arms... [omitted]

It alludes to the root idea of all our work, the projection of the Light of Universal Life through the handiwork of humanity.

The Sign of Silence is given by placing the left forefinger on the closed lips. *(Done)* It alludes to the strict silence inculcated upon you by your obligation regarding all proceedings of the Order.

The grip or token is given in the following manner. Advance your left foot about six inches, touching mine side to side and toe to heel. Extend your right hand, and grasp mine, locking the fingertips... [omitted]

Observe that the person giving the grip, as I do now, is always the first to... [omitted]

This is the distinguishing grip of the Neophyte Grade. It refers to the ten emanations of the Life-Power, the alternate rise and fall of the Fire-force, and the interchange of power and sympathy between Fellow Initiates. *(Continues to hold grip.)*

The word is _____. It is whispered mouth to ear. It signifies _____, the object of our quest and the pattern of our actions.

The present password is _____. This is changed at each Equinox.

BETWEEN THE PILLARS

H-r: *Moves straight back from the position between the Pillars to a position midway between EA and the Pillars, facing Neophyte.*

A-n: *I now place you between the Gates of the North and South, in the symbolic portal of occult science.*

A-n: *Still holding Neophyte's hand in the completed grip, A-n backs toward the East, drawing the Neophyte forward to a position midway between the Pillars. Hands are then unclasped. A-n tells Neophyte to remain there, and if A-n is 2nd Order, goes round the white pillar with the Sun and crosses the Temple, behind the Neophyte, to the former position, West of the black pillar, facing West. If A-n is in 1st Order, then he/she brings Neophyte to the position between the pillars but does not pass through them and instead goes directly across to the Black Pillar. Takes the sword from P-r.*

FINAL PURIFICATION

A-n: Let the fourth and final purification and consecration of the Neophyte take place.

H-r: *Raises lamp and staff upward at his/her side at the words of purification and again at the words of consecration, lowering them each time as soon as the formula is completed.*

P-r: *Goes diagonally to Neophyte and faces Neophyte. Signs Neophyte with water, as before, saying:*

(Frater/Soror) _____, I purify thee finally by water.

H-r: *As before, raises staff perpendicularly, white end uppermost, held by the center in the right hand. At the same time, raises the lamp with the left hand. Lowers them at the end of P-r's words.*

P-r: *Faces East and sprinkles as in Opening, but in silence. Proceeds in the Sun's course to the C-n station, faces South and sprinkles in silence. Moves to a point halfway between Neophyte and Altar, faces West and sprinkles in silence. Completes the action by moving to a point facing P-r's station and sprinkles there in silence. Sits.*

FINAL CONSECRATION

C-n: *Crosses Temple to North and goes with the Sun to a position east of and facing Neophyte. Censes Neophyte as before, saying:*

(Frater/Soror) ____, I consecrate thee finally with fire.

H-r: *(Raises and lowers staff and lamp.)*

C-n: *Goes between Neophyte and white pillar, to a position midway between Neophyte and Altar, faces West and censes silently toward the West. Goes with the Sun to P-r's station, faces North, and censes silently. Continue with Sun to East, faces East, and censes toward East. Completes the action by going with the Sun to own station, facing South and censing there. Sits.*

INVESTITURE

EA: (Frater/Soror) A-t, the fourth and final purification and consecration of the Neophyte having been accomplished, I command you to remove the rope from (his/her) waist, and the black robe it fastens, last remaining symbols of the Path of Darkness; to receive from (him/her) the step, signs, grip, word, present password of this grade; and to invest (him/her) with the apron of an Initiate.

A-t: *Hands scepter to C-n and passes directly north to the Station of the P-r, around the black pillar, then to a position directly before the Neophyte. Removes rope and black robe and hands them to C-n.*

In the following questions, A-t takes care to correct any errors made by the Neophyte.

A-t: Give me the step of Neophyte. *(Done.)*
Give me the Sign of Projected Light. *(Done.)*
Give me the Sign of Silence. *(Done.)*
Answer this sign.

Gives Sign of Projected Light. Neophyte answers with the Sign of Silence or, if necessary, A-t prompts:

A-t: The Sign of Projected Light is always answered by the Sign of Silence.

Give me the Grip or Token. *Done. A-t retains the grip for the next two questions.*

Give me the Word of this Grade. *(Done.)*
Give me the present password. *(Done.)*

A-t: *(Receives apron from C-n)*

By command of the EA, I now invest you with the apron of an Initiate. It is a key to many mysteries of our Order, which will open to you as you advance through the Grades. By its measurements, it commemorates the ideas of Unity, Love, and Understanding. Its blue color represents the evening sky...
[description omitted]

Wear this apron, beloved (Frater/Soror), in remembrance of its meaning, and let its symbolic lessons guide you henceforth.

A-t: *Assists Neophyte to put on the apron, then returns to a position west of the white pillar.*

H-r: *Passes south of white pillar and conducts Neophyte to the west side of the altar, facing East.*

EA'S LECTURE

EA: *Stands and steps to position before the throne without the scepter.*

You now behold the EA of this Temple, approaching on the step of Neophyte *(takes the step)*, in the Sign of Projected Light *(gives it)*, and admonishing you to secrecy by the Sign of Silence *(gives it)*.[9]

EA: *Continues down the middle of the Temple to a point just east of the altar.*

C-n: *Once EA has passed, replace A-t's chair and pedestal in their usual place between the Pillars.*

A-t: *Immediately assumes station but remains standing.*

A-n: *During the following speech of the EA, A-n goes round the Temple, with the Sun, to the station in the West.*

A-n/A-t: *(Together, sit.)*

EA: (Frater/Soror) _____, I congratulate you on having passed with fortitude through the ceremony of your admission into _____ Lodge No. _____, as a Neophyte of *(name of organization)*_____.

The secret name of this Order is concealed from the First Order, as from the profane, by the initials _. _. _.[7] The name is known to members of the Second Order only, but even its initials must be hidden by you from the outside world.

I now direct your attention to a brief explanation of the principal symbols of this Grade.

The hoodwink placed over your eyes at your preparation represented the darkness of ignorance. It blinded you to your true spiritual nature, symbolized by the white robe with which you were then invested. Over the white robe, you wore a black gown, symbolizing the accumulated prejudices and errors of the profane, and fastened by the rope wound three times around your waist, showing the bonds of misunderstanding which circumscribe the higher aspirations of the soul.

The altar before which you now stand is emblematical of the existing universe. It is represented in black to show the darkness and obscurity of Nature in her workings. Of its five visible sides, those facing the cardinal points are draped in the colors of the four elements, and bear the symbols of the four fixed signs of the Zodiac.

The white triangle on the altar symbolizes the Divine Light, the Creative Spirit, which forms the Universe in darkness. It, therefore, represents light dawning in darkness.

The red cross, which in this Grade surmounts the triangle, is formed by opening out the six sides of a cube. It symbolizes Life and Action but has more profound meanings, which will be explained to you as you advance to higher Grades of our fraternity.

The rose above the cross, to the East, typifies the human soul and its manifold desires, and it is also a symbol of the element of air.

Bread and salt are types of earth whence comes our sustenance. The red lamp is an emblem of the universal fire, veiled in forms of earth. The cup of the P-r symbolizes the elemental water of purification.

The mystic words, *Khabs Am Pekht,* which you heard shortly after you were brought to light, are the Egyptian originals of the Greek *Konx Om Pax,* used in the Eleusinian Mysteries. Their literal translation is: "Light in Extension," and their import is: "May Light be extended upon you."

Let the Neophyte be conducted to the East of the altar.

H-r: *Conducts Neophyte, with Sun, to East of the altar, facing East.*

EA: The station of the P-r in the North represents the powers of cold and moisture.

That of the C-n in the South marks the powers of heat and dryness.

The two pillars are those of Hermes and Solomon. They symbolize eternal equilibrium, Severity and Mercy, active and passive, fixed and volatile, and the phenomena of the dual polarity of the magnet. Through the knowledge of their equilibrium lies the pathway to Occult Science.

Therefore, I came between them to aid in your Restoration unto the Light. Therefore, you were placed between them on receiving the Secret Signs of this Grade and for your final purification and consecration.

Two contending forces, and one which unites them eternally. Two basal angles of the triangle and one which forms the apex. Such is the origin of creation, O Neophyte; such is the triad of life.

Let the Neophyte be conducted to the North.

EA: *Returns to the throne and sits.*

H-r: *Conducts Neophyte to North, facing South, and indicates with staff the stations, as they are named.*

EA: My throne in the East symbolizes the rising of Life and Light. The throne of the A-n, facing me in the West, is an emblem of increase of darkness and decrease of light. The A-t in the center synthesizes our equilibrium and the reconciler between light and darkness.

The staff and lamp of the H-r are the Magic Wand and the Light of Occult Science, to guide us through the darkness.

I have the pleasure of now instructing the H-r to announce that you have been duly admitted to the company of Initiates of *(name of organization)*_____.

(Frater/Soror) H-r, I command you to declare that the Neophyte has been duly admitted to participation in the secrets and mysteries of this Grade.

PROCLAMATION

H-r: *Leaves Neophyte, telling him/her to remain where he/she is, and goes to the right front of EA's throne, salutes the EA, turns with the Sun to face West, raises staff perpendicularly as in the Opening, and says:*

H-r: In the Name of the Lord of the Universe and by command of the EA, hear ye all! I proclaim that _____ has been admitted in due form to the company of Initiates of (name of organization)_____.

All: *Strike hands sharply together in unison, taking time from A-t.*

EA: Conduct the Neophyte to the West.

H-r: *Returns to North, passing round Temple with the Sun, to the station of the C-n, and crossing there, between A-t and Altar. Conducts Neophyte with the Sun around the Temple to position west of the altar, facing A-n.*

A-n's ADDRESS

EA: Honored A-n, I delegate to you the duty of pronouncing a short address to our (Frater/Soror) on (his/her) admission.

A-n: *(Rises.)* (Frater/Soror) _____, you have now passed through the ceremonies of your admission. I congratulate you on being admitted to this honorable Order, whose proposed object is the practical study of Occult Science.

Therefore, let me advise you to remember this day as a marked one in your existence and to adopt and cultivate a mental attitude worthy of this Order.

To this end, let me first earnestly recommend you never to forget due honor and reverence to the Lord of the Universe, for, as the whole is greater than its parts, so is that Vast One far greater than we, whose existence is derived from that Fountain of Insupportable Light, which none may name or define.

It is written that the borders of His garment of flame sweep the ends of the Universe, that from Him proceed all things, and that to Him all return. Therefore, do we adore Him and invoke Him; therefore, all our work begins in adoration of Him.

Secondly, never ridicule nor cast obloquy upon the form of religion professed by others; for what right have you to desecrate that which is sacred in their eyes?

Thirdly, never let the seal of secrecy regarding this Order be absent from your recollection, and beware, you betray it not by a casual or unthinking word.

Fourthly, study well that Great Arcanum, the true equilibrium of Severity and Mercy, for either unbalanced, is not good. Unbalanced Severity is cruelty and oppression; unbalanced Mercy is but weakness and would permit error to exist unchecked, thus making itself, as it were, the accomplice of evil.

Lastly, be not daunted by the difficulties of the occult path, and remember the power of perseverance. *(Sits.)*

EA: Let the Neophyte be conducted to the East.

H-r: *Leads Neophyte, with the Sun, to the foot of EA's throne, facing EA*

EA'S FINAL INSTRUCTION

EA: Before you may pass on to the next highest Grade of this Order, you must commit to memory rudiments of Occult Knowledge and have passed with satisfaction to your Chiefs the examination for this Neophyte Grade.

The books of ritual, the Knowledge Lecture, and the Explanatory Lectures will be given to you by the C-s when you sign your name to the roster of this Lodge.

You are expected to make the required proficiency within six months of your initiation. Attendance at our meetings is also expected unless unavoidable circumstances prevent your coming, in which case you should notify the C-s in advance.

A thorough study of the rituals and of the lectures is recommended. Thus, you will properly lay the foundation of knowledge and training on which all your subsequent building is raised.

H-r: *Faces Neophyte to the West.*

EA: Fratres et Sorores of the (*name of organization*)_____, salute our newly admitted (Frater/Soror) with the signs and welcome (him/her) into our company.

All: *Rise, following the lead of the EA, give both signs and say together:*

All: Hail awakened one! May light be extended upon you.

EA: Conduct the Neophyte to (his/her) place.

All: *All remain standing.*

H-r: *Conducts Neophyte to the seat in the northeast, nearest the station of P-r, taking him/her around the Temple in the course of the Sun.*

New Neophyte sits.

Then, EA sits.

All sit but H-r.

ASPIRATION NAME

EA: (Frater/Soror) H-r, present to the Neophyte the tray of Aspiration names for selection.

H-r: *Rises, salutes, and proceeds to carry out the instruction by walking directly to the Neophyte sitting in the 0 = 0 section of the Temple and presents the tray with several plain envelopes, each containing a single name of aspiration. The Neophyte will randomly select one envelope and give it to the H-r without opening it. If more than one member selects a motto, the H-r correctly identifies the selected envelope(s) given to him/her to avoid confusing the selection. H-r remains before the Neophyte for further instruction from the EA.*

EA: *Upon completion of selection and identification of selected envelopes by the H-r, says:*

EA: Bring the selected name(s) of Aspiration to me.

H-r: *Takes the selected envelope(s) to the EA, walking directly to the throne; gives the selected envelope(s) to the EA; then returns to station, following the course of the Sun.*

EA: (*Opens envelope.*) Fratres et Sorores, our (Frater/Soror) _____, having attained that station on the Way of Return where it is fitting to formulate the Aspiration of (his/her) Soul, is henceforth to be known and addressed among us as (Frater/Soror) _____ _____, which signifies _____. May the Lord of the Universe aid and guide (him/her) in (his/her) endeavors to build a Temple of Service on this foundation.

Repeats *this speech and the one that follows for each Neophyte if there is more than one.*

All: And may Light be extended upon you.

EA: *
A-n: *
A-t: *

RECESS

EA: *Declares a recess so that the newly initiated Neophyte(s) can be greeted and instructed on participating in the Mystic Repast.*

EA: * * I now declare a suspension of work in this Temple until the Initiates are recalled to their stations and places by the H-r.

END OF INITIATION CEREMONY

CHAPTER 2 Notes

[1] שער הפרס חכמה

שער	הפרס	חכמה
Sha.ar	ha.p'ras	Chokmah
Gate	(the) reward, prize.	Wisdom

[2] Note that after the obligation, the candidate is now a neophyte.

[3] Formation of the triangle with the P-r, C-n, and H-r During the circumambulation, the 3 officers move in unison to keep the triangle formation around the candidate. This is to protect the candidate from negative influences.

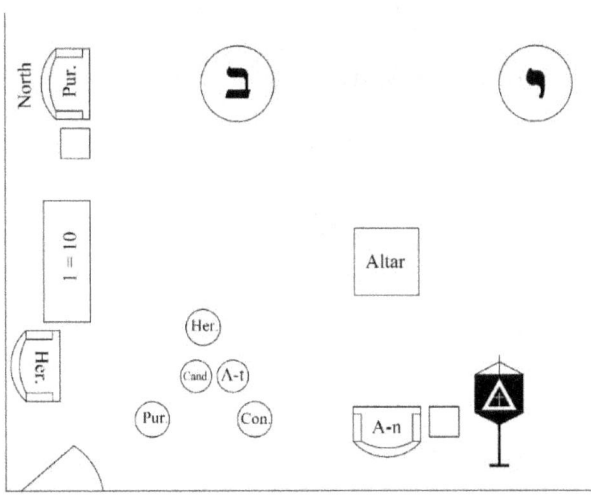

The A-t is holding the arm of the blindfolded candidate. When the P-r moves to the front of the formation to purify the candidate, the H-r moves to the place of the C-n, and the C-n moves to the P-r spot.

The three officers rotate again when it's the C-n turn to consecrate the candidate. Once the C-n finishes, the three officers rotate to their original position.

Even though the H-r is the head of the procession, the A-t has to maneuver the blindfolded candidate to the altar and around the temple. This requires the H-r leading to have eyes in the back of their head.

[4] Words in **Bold** are chanted on a single note.

[5] It is okay for the H-r to be several feet in front of the A-t who is leading the candidate. The candidate must be at the altar when the word **return** is chanted. Give the A-t and candidate plenty of room.

[6] Even though the candidate is blindfolded, it is best to memorize this speech. With each line, step towards the candidate so your voice grows in size without increasing volume. The EA should arrive at the altar when "Healing in its Wings" are spoken.

[7] The three letters and their chant are omitted.

[8] The first letter of the A-n's part is given.

[9] It is best to practice and memorize this speech to give the maximum impression on the initiate.

CHAPTER 3

THE EQUINOX

EQUINOX OPENING CEREMONY

PROCLAMATION

ANTIPHONY

RESIGNATION OF OFFICE

ADORATION TO LORD OF THE ELEMENTS

SEMESTER PASSWORD

ASSUMPTION OF OFFICE

EA's CONFESSION

PURIFICATION

CONSECRATION

MYSTIC CIRCUMAMBULATION

INVOCATION

DECLARATION

MYSTIC WORDS

THE SIGNS

RECESS

END OF OPENING

CLOSING CEREMONY

The Closing Ceremony is the same for each ritual.

THE SIGNS

PURIFICATION

CONSECRATION

LIGHT AND SOUND

REVERSE CIRCUMAMBULATION

ADORATION

MYSTIC REPAST

MYSTIC WORDS

DECLARATION

       END OF CLOSING

Similarities Between the Two Rituals

The Paul Foster Case Equinox Ritual is similar to the Golden Dawn's until the EA's Confession.

1. The PROCLAMATION is very similar in the two rituals.

2. The words of the ANTIPHONY are precisely the same.

3. The words of the RESIGNATION and ADORATION TO LORD OF THE ELEMENTS are almost identical.

4. Both rituals give a new SEMESTER PASSWORD.

5. The structure of the ASSUMPTION OF OFFICE is the same, but the GD is more elaborate.

6. Except for two words, the EA's CONFESSION is the same in the GD and PFC rituals.

Differences Between the Two Rituals

1. In the PROCLAMATION, the GD ritual nullifies the semester password.

2. In the ANTIPHONY, all give the signs to the altar in the GD ritual. However, only the officers give signs to the center in the PFC ritual, while A-t gives to the altar. This emphasizes the equal arm cross imagery.

3. In the PFC RESIGNATION OF OFFICE, the lamens are resigned with the implements of officers and left on the altar. A small table is draped with a black cloth to match the altar for extra space. Otherwise, everything is carefully stacked on the altar. This requires practice.

4. The PFC ritual gives special attention to announcing the Equinox and then giving the SEMESTER PASSWORD.

5. In the GD ritual, first, the Hierophant (EA) is installed by the Chiefs. Then the Hierophant is called upon to make his CONFESSION. Afterward, the other new officers claim their implements of office.

6. The GD Equinox Ceremony ends after the ASSUMPTION OF OFFICE.

RITUAL OF THE EQUINOX

שער הפרס חכמה

OPENING

This Opening Ceremony will be used in place of the regular 0=0 Opening at the meeting held at Equinox or a day following/preceding the Equinox, whichever is convenient. In any case, it must be held within a week of the Equinox. The Closing is the same as the regular 0=0 Closing.

Before the meeting, the H-r arranges furniture as in 0=0 Opening, except that the Cup of the P-r is placed on the Triangle on the altar. Then, when H-r has notified EA that all is ready and has opened the portal (or portals), the members should line up to enter. The order of entrance is: P-r; C-n carrying censer; A-t; A-n; Senior 4=7 members; 0=0 members; 1=10 members; Junior 4=7 members; 3=8 members; and 2=9 members.

H-r: *Opens portal and returns to the first station, facing North if the Portal is in the South-West [or South if the Portal is in the North-West], with staff uplifted at 45° angles and lamp held at heart.*

EA: * * *   Fratres et Sorores, take your stations and places.

All:	*Members and officers enter in the order described above, passing the portal with the present Password and Neophyte Signs, and go directly to their stations or seats, where they remain standing.*
H-r:	*When all are at places, close the portal.*
EA:	Be seated.

EA: *Sits.* All: *Sit.*

EA:	V.H.H. (Frater/Soror) I-r., please perform the Lesser Banishing Ritual of the Pentagram.
L-r:	*(Performs the LBRP)*
EA:	* *(Rises)*
All:	*(Rise)*
EA:	Fratres et Sorores of the _∴_∴_∴[1], let us celebrate the festival of the (Vernal/ Autumnal) Equinox. (Frater/Soror) H-r, proclaim the fact.

PROCLAMATION

H-r:	*Goes to EA's right front, as usual, salutes as in 0=0 Opening, faces west, raises staff and says:*
	In the Name of the Lord of the Universe and by command of the EA, I proclaim the (Vernal/Autumnal) Equinox. *(Returns to station.)*
EA:	According to ancient custom, let us consecrate the return of the (Vernal/Autumnal) Equinox.

ANTIPHONY

EA:	Light	A-n:	Darkness
	East		West
	Air		Water

A-t: I am the Reconciler between them.

EA & A-n:

> Give the sign of Projected Light and the Sign of Silence to the A-t (center of the temple). A-t gives signs to the altar.

C-n:	Heat	P-r	Cold
	South		North
	Fire		Earth

A-t: I am the Reconciler between them.

P-r/C-n: *Give both signs to the A-t.*

A-t: *Gives signs towards the altar.*

EA: One Creator.

C-n: One Preserver.

A-n: One Destroyer.

P-r: One Redeemer.

A-t: One Reconciler between them.

All: All five Officers give both signs to the center of the temple (A-t's station). A-t gives signs to the altar. Officers remain standing. Members sit.

RESIGNATION OF OFFICE

Ofc.: *The outgoing officers, in turn, beginning with the EA [EA, PA, A-n, A-t, H-r, C-n, P-r, Sent.] remove their mantles and insignia of office [EA retains his/her mantle until later in the ceremony], quit their posts by the left side, and go with Sun to East of Altar, facing west. Then, except for the P-r, whose cup is already on the Triangle on the altar, each holds up their lamen and implement of office and says:*

> In the name A _ _ _ _², I resign my
> (*name of implement and lamen*).

Then, lay on the altar his/her ensign, i.e., scepter, sword, censer, and staff.

A-t: A-t stands on the south side of the altar until receiving the Lamp from the H-r.

P-r: P-r says this also, although he/she does not carry the cup to the altar.

Ofc.: *Immediately after resigning their ensign, the officers pick up one symbol from the altar. The EA takes the rose, A-n the cup, and H-r takes nothing but surrenders his/her lamp to A-t, who waits at the altar for it. EA and A-n return to stations with the Sun after leaving the insignia and taking the rose and cup. A-t returns to his/her station as soon as he/she has received H-r's lamp. H-r returns to station as soon as he/she has placed staff on the altar and surrendered his/her lamp. C-n takes the red lamp, and P-r takes bread and salt. Both return to their stations. Officers remain standing, facing as usual and holding symbols taken from the altar.*

EA: (Frater/Soror) H-r, advance to the North.

All: Members, headed by Second Order and in precedence of Grades, leave their places and form in the Northwestern quarter of the temple. H-r stands North, and others form behind H-r along the North-West side, facing East.

H-r leads them to the East, where they are arranged along the temple's East side in as many rows as necessary. H-r at the Southeast end of the front row. Following the lead of the H-r, the procession faces East.

ADORATION TO LORD OF THE ELEMENTS

EA: *(Holding rose in hand and facing west, says:)*
Let us adore the Lord of the Universe.
(Faces East and raises rose)
Holy art Thou, Lord of the Air,
Who has created the firmament!
(Makes the symbol of Aquarius ♒ with the rose. Puts rose down on pedestal.)

All.: Give both signs toward East.

EA: Faces West again.

H-r: Moves procession South to the C-n. H-r at the front line of members. Following the lead of the H-r, the procession faces South.

C-n: *(Holding Red Lamp and facing North, says:)*
Let us adore the Lord of the Universe.
(Faces South and raises red lamp.)
Holy art Thou, Lord of the Fire,
Wherein Thou has shown forth the throne of Thy Glory!
(C-n makes the sign of Leo, ♌ in the air with the lamp. Puts lamp down on pedestal.)

All: Give both signs toward the South.

C-n: *Faces North again.*

H-r: *Moves procession West, facing station of A-n. H-r at North-west end of the front line of members.*

A-n: *(Holding cup in hands and facing East says:)*
Let us adore the Lord of the Universe.
(Faces west and raises cup).
Holy art Thou, Lord of the Waters,
Whereon Thy Spirit did move at the Beginning!
*(A-n traces with the cup the symbol of Scorpio ♏.
Puts cup down on pedestal.)*

All: *Give both signs toward the west.*

A-n: *Faces East.*

H-r: *Moves procession North, facing the station of the P-r. H-r at North-East end of the front line of members.*

P-r: *(Facing South, holding paten of bread and salt, says:)*
Let us adore the Lord of the Universe.
(Faces North and raises paten of bread).
Holy art Thou, Lord of the Earth,
Which Thou has made Thy footstool!
(P-r traces symbol of Taurus ♉ with paten of bread and salt. Puts down paten on pedestal.)

All: *Give both signs toward the North.*

P-r: *Faces South again.*

All: *The members now return to their usual places, following the course of the Sun around the temple.*

H-r: *Return to station.*

All: *Face as usual.*

A-t: *(Facing West)*
Let us adore the Lord of the Universe.
(Raises up H-r's lantern and pauses.)
Holy art Thou, Who art in all things.
If I climb up into Heaven, Thou art there.
If I go down into Hell, Thou art there also.
If I take the Wings of the Morning and flee unto the uttermost parts of the Sea, even there shalt Thine Hand lead me, and thy right hand shall hold me.
If I say, Peradventure, the darkness shall cover me, even the darkness shall be Light unto Thee!

Thine is the Air with its Movement! – *EA raises implement.*
Thine is the Fire with its Flashing Flame!
– *C-n raises implement.*
Thine is the Water with its Flux and Reflux!
– *P-r raises implement.*
Thine is the Earth with its enduring Stability!
– *A-n raises implement.*

A-t makes a cross with H-r's lantern. Put the lantern on the pedestal.

All: Give both signs to the altar.[4]

Ofc.: *EA, A-n, A-t, C-n, and P-r, in turn, restore to the altar the rose, cup, H-r's lantern in the center of the altar, red lamp and bread and salt. Each officer returns to their station, moving with the Sun as soon as he/she has put his/her symbol on the altar. All stand East of the Altar, facing west, as they replace their symbols. Each officer, except EA, now returns to sit with their Grade leaving all but EA's throne vacant.*

SEMESTER PASSWORD

Pr-l: It is the time of equal day and night. When the forces of light and darkness hang in the balance. For now, it is *Equinox.*

*After speaking "Equinox," a **gong** sounds, and the Pr-l, or appointed official, waits a moment in silence and announces the new Semester Password.*

Pr-l: The word for the semester commencing on the Vernal/Autumnal Equinox, _____ (year) is _____. This new word will replace the old as the password given to the H-r upon entry to the temple at all meetings after the Equinox.

ASSUMPTION OF OFFICE

The incoming officers now go to the altar in the order of EA, PA, A-n, A-t, H-r, C-n, P-r and Sentinel, or, if the same officers retain their posts, they go one by one and take their insignia. Each officer, in turn, says:

Ofc.: By and in the name A _ _ _ _ _ _,[2] I claim my (*name of implement and lamen*).

(*Officers take their new stations.*)

(*Outgoing EA bestows mantle on incoming EA*)

All: *Sit.*

P-r: Fratres et Sorores of the Order of the _/_/_/[1], behold you're EA, installed and enthroned, and by the power in me vested, I proclaim (him/her) the Revealer of Mysteries among you for the ensuing six months, being part of that temporal period through which we are conducted into Light.

Very Honored (Frater/Soror), in the presence of the Children of your Temple, I call upon you to make your Confession.

EA'S CONFESSION

EA: *(Rises)* Fratres et Sorores of the _∴_∴_∴, seeing that the whole intention of the Lesser Mysteries, or of external initiation, is by the intervention of the Symbol, Ceremonial, and Sacrament, to lead the Soul that it may be withdrawn from the attraction of matter and delivered from the absorption therein whereby it walks in darkness, knowing not whence it cometh nor whither it goeth; and also seeing, that thus withdrawn, the Soul by true direction must be brought to study of Divine Things, that it may offer the only pure and acceptable sacrifice, which is love expressed towards God, Humanity and the Universe; now, therefore, I confess and testify thereto, from my throne in this temple, and I promise, so far as in me lies, to lead you by the Rites of this Order, faithfully conserved, and exhibited with becoming reverence, that through such love and such sacrifice, you may be prepared in due time for the greater Mysteries, the Supreme and inward Initiation. *(Sits.)*

(Frater/Soror) H-r, please see that the articles on the altar are properly arranged.

H-r: *Goes to Altar, arranges articles properly, and returns to station.*

PURIFICATION

EA: (Frater/Soror) P-r, I command you to purify the Temple and the Initiates by Water.

P-r: Advances diagonally from station to East of the temple, before the throne of EA, carrying the cup in both hands. Facing EA, P-r gives Sign of Respect, to which EA responds as usual. P-r then holds the cup at the heart center and says:

    I purify by Water.

Dips right thumb, forefinger, and middle finger held together in the cup of water and sprinkles 3 times toward the East to form the points of a water triangle:

              1   2

                  3

P-r then turns in place to face the C-n in the South and says:

    I purify by Water.

P-r sprinkles again, then faces west and say:

    I purify by Water.

Sprinkles then face their station in the North & says:

    I purify by Water.

Sprinkles a fourth time, then faces east again, gives the Sign of Respect, turns with the Sun to face their station, and walks there directly. At the station, places the cup on the pedestal, faces the EA and says:

P-r: The Temple is cleansed.
(Remains standing at station, facing south, during the consecration.)

CONSECRATION

EA: (Frater/Soror) C-n, I command you to consecrate the Temple and the Initiates with Fire.

C-n: *Prepares the censer with fresh incense. The censer should be actively smoking. Advances diagonally from station to East of the temple, before the throne of EA, carrying censer in both hands. Facing East, C-n gives the Sign of Respect, to which the EA responds. Then, holding the censer at heart level, C-n says:*

C-n: I consecrate with Fire.

C-n: *Censes with three thrusts towards the East to form the points of a fire triangle, thus:*

1

2   3

Turn in place to face your own station, and say:

    I consecrate with Fire.

Censes again, then face west and say:

    I consecrate with Fire.

Censes then face the P-r's station and say:

    I consecrate with Fire.

Censes a 4th time, faces east, gives the Sign of Respect, turns with the Sun to face their station, and walks there directly. At station, places the censer on the pedestal, faces the EA, and says:

C-n: The Temple is consecrated.
    (Remains standing at station, facing North.)

MYSTIC CIRCUMAMBULATION [3]

EA: *(Rises.)* Let the Mystic Circumambulation take place in the Path of Light.

All: *At the word "Light," all members rise and form the procession in the North.*

Formation with Members in All Grades

When the whole procession is in motion, it is in the following order: H-r, A-t, I-r, C-s, PA, 2nd Order Members, A-n, 0=0, P-r, 1=10, 2=9, C-n, 3=8, Jr. 4=7, Sr. 4=7.

EA: When officers and members have arrived at accustomed stations and places:

The mystic circumambulation is accomplished. It is symbolic of the rising Light.

EA: *Waits until the designated member goes to the light switch, switches on the light, and returns.*

EA then continues:

EA: Let us invoke the Lord of the Universe.

INVOCATION

All: *(Face East.)*

EA: *(Raises scepter.)* Be Thy Name Blessed, O Lord of the Universe, unto the Eternal Ages. Unto the members of this Order be Thou Propitious and grant them at last, the Summum Bonum, for the gift of the Perfect Wisdom, the gift of the Sacred Stone are with Thee in Thine Eternal Light, by the Power of the Secret Name.

All: **Amen.**

Members salute with both signs. Officers lower their insignia. All face as usual.

EA: (Frater/Soror) H-r, in the Name of the Lord of the Universe, I command you to declare that the (Vernal/Autumnal) Equinox has returned and that this temple has been attuned to the secret forces operating until the Equinox to come.

DECLARATION

H-r: *Advances to EA's right front, salutes as usual and faces west, holding staff aloft, says:*

In the Name of the Lord of the Universe and by command of the EA, I declare that the Sun has entered (Aries/Libra), the sign of the (Vernal/Autumnal) Equinox and that this temple has been attuned to the forces in operation for the half-year ensuing.

(H-r returns to his/her station with the Sun.)

MYSTIC WORDS

EA:	Khabs.	*
A-n:	Am.	*
A-t:	Pekht.	*
A-n:	Konx.	*
A-t:	Om.	*
EA:	Pax.	*
A-t:	Light.	*
EA:	In.	*
A-n:	Extension.	*

THE SIGNS

EA: Fratres et Sorores, the signs.

All: *Members and Officers give both signs.*

EA: *EA sits. All: sit.*

RECESS

EA: * * I now declare a suspension of work in this Lodge until the Initiates are recalled to their stations and places by the H-r.

END OF OPENING

CLOSING CEREMONY

The Equinox closing is the same as Chapter 1, Neophyte Ritual.

CHAPTER 3 Notes

[1] The letters of the Secret Name were deleted.

[2] First letter of the name is given.

[3] A detailed Mystic Circumambulation description can be found in Chapter 1 Notes.

[4] Note that the signs are given to the altar with all the officers' implements on top.

CHAPTER 4

IMPLEMENTS AND REGALIA

Chiefs

PG with scepter, lamen, and violet mantle.

Pr-l with Scepter of Unity, lamen and blue mantle.

I-r with Scepter of Pentalpha, lamen, and red mantle.

C-s with Scepter of Reconciliation, lamen, and yellow mantle.

Officers' Insignia

EA with Scepter of Dominion, lamen, and red mantle.

PA with an apron with red edging and cords.

A-n with the sword, lamen, and black mantle.

A-t with Scepter of Equilibration, lamen, and white mantle.

H-r with lamen, lamp and staff.

C-n with lamen, censer and incense.

P-r with lamen and the cup of Water

Sentinel (as needed) with lamen and sword.

Member Regalia

All members wear white robes and white shoes or socks. (I prefer socks. Feeling the temple floor under my feet grounds me.)

The PFC ceremony does not use a Nemis headdress.

The Golden Dawn cordeliere is replaced with an apron. Paul Case was a Mason, so the apron has Masonic influences.

In the PFC ritual, the officer visualizations are archangelic and based on the Tarot Keys.

Cantor

Electric keyboard or xylophone to sound musical notes.

Members

Clothed with white undergarments, white shoes, white robe, baldric depending upon grade, and apron/cordelier.

CHAPTER 5

TEMPLE SETUP

ARRANGEMENTS FOR THE OPENING AND INITIATION

Full Setup

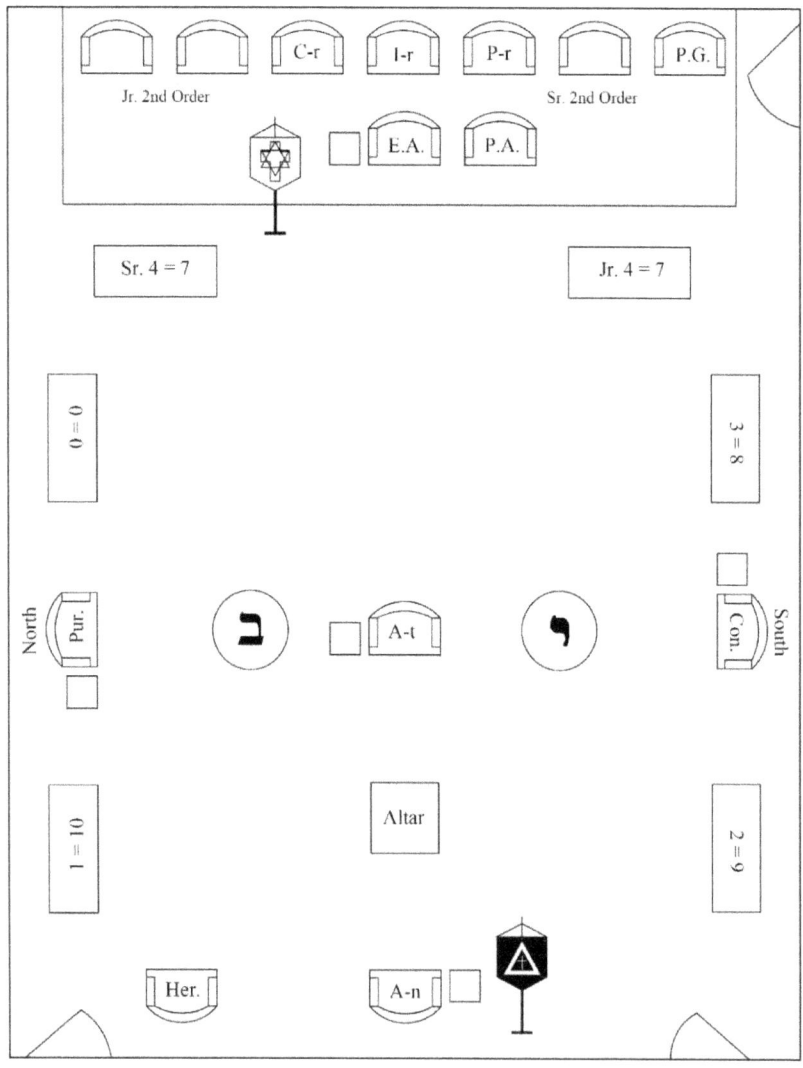

Set up for Visiting Members and the Equinox

It takes six people to open a lodge as a hall of neophytes. Typically, lodge chiefs (C-s, I-r, and Pr-l) perform the ritual and rarely sit in their actual positions, except during the Equinox Ceremony.

The rectangular box in the upper part of the drawing is a raised floor (dais) typical of Masonic lodges. In the north and south are rows of chairs where the members sit based on their grades.

PA is the Past A. This position is only used when it's the first time an individual is the EA.

The bottom-right door is the entrance used by initiates. The bottom left door is where the candidate enters.

Typical Temple Setup

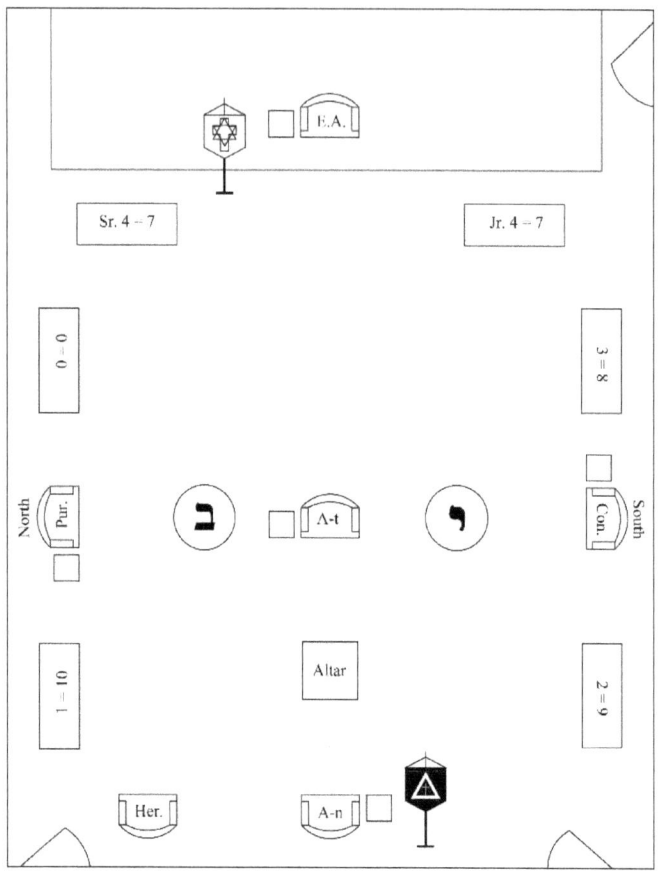

EA is in the East with a table at the right hand covered with a red cloth. (Wood TV trays are portable and at the right height.)

South is the station of the C-n, with a table at the right covered with a red cloth.

3=8 members sit facing North, East of C-n.

2=9 members sit facing North, West of C-n.

A-n in the west with a table at the right hand, covered with a black cloth.

Between the A-n and the S.W. portal is the 1st station of the H-r. H-r's 2nd station is before the closed door of the Portal. When there is a N.W. portal (bottom right), as in the diagram, H-r's place during initiation is north of A-n.

North is the station of P-r with a table at the right, covered with a blue cloth.

0=0 members sit facing South, East of the P-r.

1=10 members sit facing south, west of P-r.

A-t between the Pillars, facing West, with a table at the right covered with a white cloth.

Pillars

The Pillars are placed in the center of the Temple, midway between the stations of the EA and A-n, at the station of the A-t.

The pillars are shaped like lotus buds and usually have candles placed inside. However, a pool of melted wax can spill on your clothes or carpet when you remove the pillar capitals (top) by the end of the ceremony. Therefore, it is best to use LED lights for the pillars.

Altar

Placed halfway between the stations of the A-t and A-n. Altar cloth of four elements; a red cross and a white triangle in the center, with the cross above the triangle; a red rose in the eastern portion of the altar; a red lamp in the South; a paten of bread and salt in the North. The cup on the altar is in the West.

Banners

The Banner of the East is placed on the dais North of the EA station. The Banner of the West is placed at the right hand of the A-n.

For Initiation

Candidate with red rose, white robe, black robe over the white robe, black cordelier, hoodwink. Guide with outer black robe and black cordelier. Apron and tray of aspiration names.

For Light and Sound

Color Cards and light source.

Other Regalia

The Charter for the Lodge is placed in the Temple. The Banner of the Lodge is placed in the Temple. The Grand Lodge Banner, when used, is placed in the East.

Candles and Ritual

Most public buildings have fire codes and may restrict fire inside a temple. The candle inside the H-r's lantern is enclosed, and the light on the altar is well-contained.

The biggest fire hazard is the C-n lighting incense. The charcoal flares and casts spark that damage a rug.

Since we met in a Masonic lodge with a full kitchen, we used the gas stove to light the charcoal by holding it with tongs over a flame.

Masonic Lodge Etiquette

Do not move their lodge furniture. Much of it is antique and irreplaceable. If you use the kitchen, don't forget to remove the trash before leaving.

Cup of the P-r

A sterling silver cup is best. Silver needs cleaning, and an electroplated cup will eventually lose the silver coating. The best place to find a silver chalice is a coin shop that takes scrap silver. Occasionally they get a sterling cup. If the goblet has any engravings, take it to a jeweler, and they can buff it off.

PAUL FOSTER CASE BOOKS

1. SEVEN STEPS IN PRACTICAL OCCULTISM

2. AN INTRODUCTION TO THE TAROT AND ASTROLOGY

3. TAROT FUNDAMENTALS

4. TAROT INTERPRETATIONS

5. THE MASTER PATTERN

6. THE THIRTY-TWO PATHS OF WISDOM

7. THE TREE OF LIFE

8. THE NEOPHYTE RITUALS OF PAUL FOSTER CASE

9. THE ATTUNEMENT RITUALS OF PAUL FOSTER OF CASE

10. THE SECOND ORDER RITUALS OF PAUL FOSTER CASE

WADE COLEMAN BOOKS

1. SEPHER SAPPHIRES Volume 1

2. SEPHER SAPPHIRES Volume 2

3. THE ASTROLOGY WORKBOOK

4. MAGIC OF THE PLANETS

5. THE ZODIAC OF DENDARA EGYPT

6. THE MAGICAL PATH

7. ATHANASIUS KIRCHER'S QUADRIVIUM

To contact the author,

DENDARA_ZODIAC@protonmail.com